Writing for the Screen

D0808472

WITHDRAWN

21 FEB 2024

Approaches to Writing

Series Editor: Graeme Harper

Published

Amanda Boulter, *Writing Fiction*
Craig Batty and Zara Waldeback, *Writing for the Screen*
Chad Davidson and Greg Fraser, *Writing Poetry*

Forthcoming

Bruce Dobler, *Writing Creative Nonfiction*

Approaches to Writing
Series Standing Order
ISBN 1–4039–9999–6
(*outside North America only*)

You can receive future titles in this series as they are published by placing a standing order. Please contact your bookseller or, in case of difficulty, write to us at the address below with your name and address, the title of the series, and the ISBN quoted above.

Customer Services Department, Palgrave Macmillan Ltd,
Houndmills, Basingstoke, Hampshire RG21 6XS, England

Writing for the Screen

Creative and Critical Approaches

Craig Batty and Zara Waldeback

palgrave
macmillan

First published 2008 by
PALGRAVE MACMILLAN

Palgrave Macmillan in the UK is an imprint of Macmillan Publishers Limited, registered in England, company number 785998, of Houndmills, Basingstoke, Hampshire RG21 6XS.

Palgrave Macmillan in the US is a division of St Martin's Press LLC, 175 Fifth Avenue, New York, NY 10010.

Palgrave Macmillan is the global academic imprint of the above companies and has companies and representatives throughout the world.

Palgrave® and Macmillan® are registered trademarks in the United States, the United Kingdom, Europe and other countries.

ISBN 978-0-230-55075-9 paperback

This book is printed on paper suitable for recycling and made from fully managed and sustained forest sources. Logging, pulping and manufacturing processes are expected to conform to the environmental regulations of the country of origin.

A catalogue record for this book is available from the British Library.

A catalog record for this book is available from the Library of Congress.

Printed in Great Britain by the MPG Books Group, Bodmin and King's Lynn

Contents

Acknowledgements

Craig Batty would like to thank his Mum, Dad and Sister for all their love and support from the very start; his friends, north and south, for keeping him sane during the project and inspiring it in their own way; and academic and writing colleagues across the globe, for their invaluable help and inspiration along what has been a very exciting journey – from curious student to passionate author and lecturer.

Zara Waldeback would like to thank Britt Harrison and Karen Lee Street for being so inspiring and teaching her so much; Lighthouse, TVU and Screen South for supporting her writing; Lynette and Julie – perfect partners in crime; and all her writing group colleagues and students, who have been such willing test subjects and have helped to shape theories and teaching practices.

Both authors would like to thank Professor Graeme Harper, for belief in the project and enabling it to happen in the first place; Julian Friedmann, for continued support and enthusiasm in publishing their articles in *ScriptWriter Magazine*, some of which have formed the basis for work in this book; and the team at Palgrave Macmillan (Kate, Kitty, Felicity et al.), who have been a joy to work with from day one.

Introduction

Screenwriting is an art form unlike any of its creative writing counterparts. It shares common qualities with prose, poetry and playwriting in that it entails storytelling, plot, character, voice and tools of audience engagement, but principally it is a very particular and distinct form of writing. This may explain why, in many universities, screenwriting sits within film, television, media and communication departments rather than those of English and literary studies. The connections here may be obvious, but if screenwriting is deemed as creative writing then why is it treated as fundamentally different? Sitting within such 'modern' departments, screenwriting is probably viewed more *media writing* than *creative writing*. In this sense we might read it as a more commercial enterprise, driven by industrial and vocational factors as opposed to organic and philosophical ones. This can, however, be contested, and ideas contrary to this will be discussed later. Screenwriting teaching and training, both in academic and professional contexts, can often be more pragmatic and aware of the form's part in a *process*; a chain of development stages which move from one to the other to build the end product (film, TV drama). Unlike poets and novelists, whose work is crafted and polished to a standard ready to be published and consumed, screenwriters craft and polish screenplays which are then handed over to be cast, rehearsed, designed, shot, edited and marketed. Although other forms of creative writing operate in collaborative environments, none do so in the same way as screenwriting. The stages of production can involve hundreds of people, all working for the benefit of one piece of writing. It is perhaps no surprise then that screenwriting is viewed with much more of a financial eye; as the industry deals in 'mega bucks', if a screenplay does not work, a lot of capital is at risk. Screenwriters can earn huge amounts of money, but vision and creativity can also be stifled by commercial constraints. Nevertheless, the art of screenwriting should not be underestimated. Screenplays can take shape from very personal experiences and can be written with a very unique writer's voice and style.

The nature of screenwriting

A screenplay, whether for film or television, is a blueprint for the next stage of production; a document with words and actions ready to be realised. In many cases the screenplay can take more than a year to develop before it is ready for production; the writer effectively conceives and gives birth to a screenplay which is then passed on and 'raised' by a producer and director. In some rare instances the screenwriter is involved during production, but generally speaking the screenwriter is paid for the work then waves goodbye to the baby. This is not a negative concept, but simply an inherent part of screenwriting that has to be accepted. Due to the nature of its process it must also be understood that screenwriting is heavily reliant upon planning. Chapter 1 will outline the life of a screenplay, and often the screenwriter experiences a lengthy development process before a word of dialogue is written. Initially a screenwriter will develop an idea into a rough dramatic shape. This is then often written out as a treatment or step outline, allowing a feel for story and structure. Depending on the project, and if a producer has expressed interest, this document alone may take months to perfect. Feedback will be sought from various sources and worked into the outline of the screenplay, then drafting begins. This is a deep, lengthy process of perfecting characters, enriching dialogue and sharpening scenes and can be very collaborative, involving producers, script editors and financiers. Only when this is done can the final polish be attempted and the screenplay ready for pre-production. Aspiring screenwriters or those working speculatively (see Chapter 11) will not go through all the official stages above, but nevertheless will spend similar amounts of time developing, writing and rewriting. If a screenwriter is lucky enough to sell the idea early on, more people become involved and collaboration truly steps up. The screenplay will evolve from meeting to meeting, phone call to phone call, until all those with an interest (often financial) are happy it meets their requirements. Many screenplays are also written to suit a particular genre, which entails another set of demands on the writer and writing process. Perhaps seen as the epitome of screenwriting's business nature, genre requires that screenplays are shaped and packaged according to how the market operates to satisfy audience expectation. Genre interventions, discussed further in Chapters 6 and 13, place a huge claim on the screenwriter. This comes not only in the form of ensuring the screenplay gives the right tone or feel to an audience, but requires integral elements of the screenplay to be formulated to suit: story, structure, character, visual grammar. These commercial and social constraints are not entirely negative, however; they can have value for a screenwriter, as Lucy Scher, of UK training organisation The Script Factory outlines:

> An understanding of genre gives you confidence. If a script is really hitting the mark, I'll bet that it is working because you know what you would expect in this kind of story and it is being delivered with enough freshness to get you excited. If the screenplay is not really hitting the mark, which is perhaps more likely, an understanding of genre can inform your thinking about what you are expecting and how this story is at variance from those expectations.
>
> (2003: para 15)

The fabric of screenwriting

Screenwriting does exactly what it promises – writes for the screen. Stories are told in what is mainly a visual medium, and so what is *seen* by the audience is of paramount importance. Dialogue and voice is in no way to be discredited (see Chapters 5 and 12), but the power of the visual image is something to be fully aware of. Many developing screenwriters begin with scripts that sound more like radio or theatre plays, heavy in dialogue with little attention to how the screen can be used to tell the story. Charlie Moritz points out that '[p]arallels have often been drawn between watching screen dramas... and the experience of dreaming... wherever possible, the pictures and the action should always come first. It is what we are watching which truly engages our interest' (2001: 47). We all see and we all dream; yet when writing screenplays the focus is often on what we say. If a screenwriter can take that leap into the visual, negotiating the relationship between what an audience sees and what it hears, a new level is reached. Deeper, richer and more professional screenplays are written by those who understand the capacity of the frame, filling it with visual texture and meaning.

A screenplay is a moment in time; a story told in a particular temporal frame. The narrative unfolds in the eyes, ears and imagination of the audience who engages with the characters and situations presented. It is a psychosomatic experience, as Grodal asserts:

> The film [and television] experience is made up of many activities: our eyes and ears pick up and analyze image and sound, our minds apprehend the story, which resonates on our memory; furthermore, our stomach, heart, and skin are activated in empathy with the story situations and the protagonists' ability to cope.
>
> (1997: 1)

A plot unfolds in front of the audience's eyes, shaped carefully to tell a story which will leave them with resonance. The story is always one of human action and behaviour, and the deeper meaning that stems from this; action and reaction; doing and feeling. This is the essence of a screenplay. We could almost go a step further and say that the screenplay is a living organism; it breathes; lives; is always active. This personification works well because it gives the screenplay the status of a human being, something we see and hear in our everyday life, which embodies life itself. Screenwriters construct screenplays not only because they enjoy going to the cinema or watching TV, but because they have something to say; the screenplay pulls it to life. Robert McKee provides some interesting thoughts:

> Our appetite for story is a reflection of the profound human need to grasp the patterns of living, not merely as an intellectual exercise, but within a very personal, emotional experience. In the words of playwright Jean Anouilh, "Fiction gives life its form." [...] Story isn't a flight from reality but a vehicle that carries us on our search for reality, our best effort to make sense out of the anarchy of existence.
>
> (1999: 12)

Screenwriting's fabric, the vehicle to tell the story, is structure. Structure is used to shape ideas into a usable, watchable and understandable form for the audience. The screenplay as a whole is the macro structure; it holds everything together (see Chapter 3). Within this is the micro; smaller parts which form the whole, including acts, sequences, scenes, characters, action, dialogue, gesture, utterance and silence. From biggest to smallest, they create the complete narrative which captures the moment in time that is a screenplay. It is essential to understand the idea of cause and effect; how a character's action leads to another character's reaction, and subsequently the taking of another action. Generally speaking things do not 'just happen,' so the fabric of a screenplay relies upon an awareness of the cause and effect relationship. Like atoms, characters and voices collide and spin off in other directions, colliding once more and so on. From these, decisions are made which inform the next set of collisions. This raises a crucial notion of screenwriting: conflict. The very fabric of a screenplay feeds upon character and action conflict; characters being stopped from getting what they want. This is a fundamental idea which all screenwriters have to be aware of. If there is no conflict, there is no drama. However, it is important to also consider what makes *meaningful* conflict in order to create a full, rich, emotional experience from the series of collisions; conflict *and* connection (see Chapter 2).

The layout of a screenplay

The formatting of a screenplay is crucial to get right for two important reasons. Not only will work sent to agents, production companies or competitions only be read if in professional format, the format itself gives a reasonably accurate sense of screen time; one page equals one minute. The standard screenplay layout contains: the slugline (another word for scene heading), and tells if a scene is set inside (Int.) or outside (Ext.) along with scene location and time of day; scene action, which details what is physically happening within the scene; character name so we know who is speaking; and dialogue, the words the audience will hear, occasionally with a suggestion (in brackets) of how the line is said, if it is not obvious from the words (to be used very sparingly). Occasionally scene transitions are stated at the end of a scene, such as fade to and dissolve to. The general advice here is that unless the transition has to be specific, then nothing needs to be said; a cut to is implied with the start of a new scene. A typical screenplay layout might look something like this.

```
INT. HOUSE - KITCHEN - EVENING

JANE pours the tea as TOM sits waiting. The silence
is awkward.

TOM goes to say something but thinks better of it.
JANE puts the tea in front of him. She can't look
him in the eye.

                    TOM
          I guess you...did it arrive then?

JANE looks at TOM then away again.

                    TOM
          You don't have to pretend...

                    JANE
                    (flips)
          How d'you think it felt?

TOM quietly puts his tea down and walks away. JANE
puts her hands to her face.
```

Screenwriters today are lucky in that formatting packages are widely available, *Final Draft* being the most common. However, to avoid the somewhat high cost, another useful package is the BBC's *ScriptSmart*. This gives the same layout, and allows settings to be changed between screen, stage, radio and prose. *ScriptSmart* is available free of charge from www.bbc.co.uk/writersroom; so do not give script readers an excuse to dismiss work before they have read it.

Now that we have laid some of the key foundations of the art of screenwriting, preparing readers for the exciting yet tumultuous world that is the film and television industry, we would like to outline more about what this book intends to do. Moving away from simple 'how to' approaches found in many popular publications, this book aims to link creativity in practice with ways to increase critical awareness of this practice and its results, offering challenging and stimulating creative-critical debates.

Creative approaches to screenwriting

Traditionally, screenwriting has come to be viewed as a mainly 'mechanical' form of writing, centring on structural architecture and craft skill; commercial and formulaic as opposed to organic and creative. Story conferences, script editing meetings and much script training focuses on how to build a script rather than examine the process of coming to the idea. Such seemingly 'mechanical' issues have their uses but have overshadowed other equally important aspects. Even the way in which screenwriting is taught focuses more on craft and rules than imagination and creativity (examined in Chapter 13). From our experiences of working in development, it has become clear that many scripts are well written, but often tell unexciting or over-familiar stories. It is our view that many of these problems arise because of a lack of attention to the creative rather than mechanical process in screenwriting development. Fiction writers and poets often have a good working relationship (or at least understanding) of the process that comes before the actual production of writing, the more nebulous time akin to daydreaming, drifting, experimenting and playing. It is the theme, story and emotion at the centre of a script which ensures its success, not just the technical manner in which it is constructed, and screenwriting is in danger of losing its heart if we do not reintroduce notions of creativity into its practice. Screenwriters need to understand how to have ideas, what creative processes suit them, why they get stuck, why they come to be a writer and what they really have to say. Most screenwriting guides offer variations of paradigms, principles, check lists and trouble-shooting exercises to make the screenplay take shape. These are very useful, and this book will offer some of its own, but what we aim to develop differently is a sense of creativity within screenwriting. The screenplay may be a form driven by commercial factors, and more than other creative writing is reliant upon shape and structure, but that does not mean the screenwriter's creativity should be ignored.

Critical approaches to screenwriting

Critical appraisal of screenwriting is still an emerging discipline. Film and television 'theory' has existed for decades, and much of screenwriting's critical theory draws from this. However, film and television theory is not screenwriting theory. Screenwriting theory has its own unique position and its own concerns. It is not a case of bolting-on established theory in the hope that links to writing can be deduced; rather, it is an opportunity to create (and relocate) knowledge specifically dedicated to the art and craft of screenwriting. What we should be aiming to attain is, as Harper suggests, a 'site of knowledge' (2006: 3)[1] focused upon screenwriting (as part of creative and media writing) as a discipline in itself. The subsequent development of 'creative theory' around the subject seeks not to reject theories or critical insights which may be useful, but rather attempt to 'absorb theoretical critical positions, which are already established in most ... [Higher Education] institutions, with [an ultimate] view to producing better writers' (Melrose, 2007: 110).

For these reasons, we would like to treat screenwriting as an academic discipline with its own (growing) critical space. Because we are dealing with a *practice* rather than a *theory*, some of this critical knowledge will be distinctive in approach. Rather than purely offering ways of academically assessing end product, sometimes it is highly relevant to assess and analyse process and procedure. As highlighted, screenwriting is an *active* form and screenplays are *living* products. Therefore, screenwriting theory should concern itself with *activating* the form and *living* with the product. It is our hope that the critical insights offered throughout this book will challenge and stimulate writers and their writing process. Writers who are critically aware of their discipline and their position within that discipline can be better writers. Similarly perhaps, critical thinkers who are creatively aware of their discipline and can practise that discipline can become better critical thinkers. For screenwriters in particular, critical appraisal should not be seen as an ancillary, 'post event' process, but one which is drawn upon and used throughout the practice: before (ideas gathering, inspiration, development), during (screenplay writing and rewriting) and after (editing, viewing, reflecting).

Using the book

In *Foundations*, we will introduce creative and critical ideas which occupy the more recognised aspects of creative practice and critical understanding of screenwriting. These ideas include subject and character, structure and narrative, visual storytelling and dialogue. In *Speculations* we will offer alternative and comparative ways of seeing, writing and contextualising practice and critical understanding. Drawing upon areas such as cultural studies, visual studies and psychology, areas of speculation include alternative narrative structures, challenges to the creative process, character arcs and ideology and notions of truth and reality in factual drama. At the end of both *Foundations* and *Speculations*, exercises are provided to complement the areas discussed, guiding you through creative processes and critical analyses in order to have a positive impact upon your development both as writer and learner. The best way to use this book is to be interactive and make links between chapters, finding ways in which discussions of one topic help with the understanding of another, and to regard the book as a whole; working through it as best suits your process, then revisiting individual chapters for specialist advice and development help.

We hope you find the book interesting, insightful and most of all, useful. Good luck – and here's to creating better screenwriters!

Part I

Foundations

1 Establishing Practice

There are a number of practical issues that affect the life of a screenwriter and make it distinctly different from that of other creative writers. The screenwriter has to strike a balance between working independently, with discipline and creativity, in isolation, and working effectively with producers, script editors, directors and promoting themselves through networking and pitching. The development of a script tends to follow a rather prescribed path, and screenwriters have to learn how to work to brief, react to notes, deliver drafts to deadlines and offer work in a number of forms, such as pitches, treatments and step outlines. It is therefore imperative that the screenwriter establishes a sense of creative practice to help maintain a sense of focus among a potentially convoluted process, where many voices enter the fray to offer comments and demand changes, not always with great insight or knowledge.

A screenplay normally comes into being as one of the following:

(1) *Spec Script* – a writer chooses to develop an original idea and write it without having been asked or paid to do so, that is, writes 'speculatively' ('on spec');
(2) *Commission* – a producer hires a writer to create a script of an idea, often from an outside source, such as the producer himself, or another party;
(3) *Adaptation* – the writer adapts pre-existing work such as a novel or play into a script, often at the request of a producer.

In the UK the most common way for screenwriters to make a living is through commissions and adaptations. The spec script plays a negligible though important part of a writer's career; it often serves as the sample that gets the writer a commission, and some original scripts do get produced. They also help develop the writer's voice, that freshness development executives and producers often look for in emerging writers. In Hollywood, there has traditionally been more of a market for the spec script, as described by Taylor: 'The security of Hollywood's bygone era no longer remains, but has been replaced by the insecurities

of a new studio system that feeds off the screenwriters' original material'
(1999: 7). Recently, however, the American industry is also focusing
on adaptations, which, with their established target markets of pre-
existing products (novels, comics, games, TV shows) are seen to carry
less financial risk.

The development process

Development refers to the phase after the idea has been selected until
final script is delivered. For Sendall, '[d]evelopment isn't the complication of matters but their simplification... Simplifying actually creates
deeper, complex layers; complicating creates superficial ones' (2003: 9).
In other words, development is not a convoluted, bureaucratic process
but one which enables the writer to fully understand their project and
allows a richer script to grow. Therefore development is the mainstay
of a script's life cycle, and moves through a number of stages. These
include, though not necessarily all, nor in this order:

- Pitch
- Outline
- Treatment
- Step Outline
- First Draft Script
- Number of draft versions of Script (anything up to twenty or
  beyond)
- Final Draft Script

It is useful to think of development not as a linear but circular (or spiral)
process. The writer may start off with a pitch or outline, then complete
a draft, step outline, another two or three script drafts, return to working with a new step outline, revise the pitch and sales treatment and
complete a final script. Each project requires it owns working process
and it is important not to get locked into a rigid model.

When writers or producers want to sell or raise interest in scripts,
they often produce documents so financiers do not have to read a
whole script without knowing if it might be something they are interested in. This is commonplace in the UK and Europe, though less so in
Hollywood. As well as sales tools, these concentrated versions can also
help the creative work during development. Different documents serve
different purposes and the terminology can sometimes be confusing

as industry professionals do not always share the same language. There-fore writers are always advised to ask how many pages is expected to make sure they offer documents in a format palatable to the potential buyer.

A *treatment* is a selling document, anything from three to thirty pages. A prose version of the script, it reads in a clear and engaging manner. It should have a strong sense of beginning, middle and end without giving too many details and does not usually include dialogue. It should introduce all main characters in a concise, dynamic way and suggest both theme and world. The purpose of a treatment is usually to get the reader to either commission a script or read the existing draft and it is therefore essential that it is a polished piece of work in the right tone, where reading the treatment gives a similar feeling to watching the eventual film. If it is a horror, the treatment should be frightening; if a thriller, tense; if a comedy, funny.

A *story outline* is often very similar to a treatment but there are two potential differences: an outline is usually shorter, sometimes just a page or two, and often more of a working document rather than a selling one. However, industry professionals tend to use these terms interchangeably and there is no big difference between them. As a working document, created either before or after script drafts, it can help clarify structure, character arcs and plotting, and can be useful during development.

A *synopsis* is a summary of the plot. Often quite short (no more than a page or two) and similar to an outline, it tends to be written after the story is completed, often by a script reader in a report (coverage) or for marketing purposes. It summarises the story in a dispassionate description of main events and characters. It can be very useful for a writer to read a synopsis of their story written by someone else as it demonstrates how the story is coming across and if there are moments, themes or characters that are not communicating as intended.

A *step outline* is always a working document, never used to sell the script. It is a bare-bones outline, breaking down each scene into key 'steps' in order to show how the story connects together. Not concerned with presenting it in a polished manner, it simply details the facts and emotions to highlight story architecture. It can be an extremely help-ful document at many points in the development process as it allows the writer to stand back from detail and see how pieces of the puzzle fit into the bigger picture. In a step outline, each scene is represented by a scene heading and a two to three line plain description of what happens, both in terms of plot and emotion, and any key changes that take place. It reduces each step to its most essential elements to clarify the purpose of the scene and does not include dialogue or description. Instead, it highlights the reason for each scene's inclusion in the story, and by doing this the writer can decide which scenes are redundant, which can be condensed and combined, or how to improve the order.

Using *index cards* is an effective tool for working with structure, moving beyond initial story assumptions to discover new ideas and solve problems. As with step outlines, working with cards gets to the heart of a story quickly, and allows writers to test a large number of ideas without wasting time writing them out as full versions. Cards allow the writer to see as many possibilities as they can in the story, which can then be combined in more innovative, fresh, surprising and appropriate ways. The main beat of a scene is written on each card, and they are laid out on a floor or displayed on a wall to experiment with different scene orders. It is extremely useful to know the purpose of each scene as it will allow the writer to build and analyse story architecture with a great degree of precision. During the writing of the script, knowing the purpose of each scene is invaluable, and working with cards can highlight problems with pace, plot and structure at an early stage.

The *sequence outline* is a working (not selling) tool mainly used in feature development. As these are large sprawling narratives, writers need to gain an overview quickly and effectively. Nearly all features are divided up into eight sequences and this 'road map', outlining each sequence in brief paragraphs, analyses how key building blocks combine to produce rising action, thematic resonance and narrative momentum. It can also be an excellent place to start building story as it quickly demonstrates whether there is enough 'fuel in the tank' in the premise. Chapter 3 discusses in-depth the use of sequences as a structural tool.

Treatments, step outlines, index cards and sequence outlines are all crucial tools of the development process and should be used as and when needed. Part of becoming an experienced screenwriter is to learn which tool is appropriate at what time in order to create an effective development process, as it will differ from writer to writer and project to project. A key to understanding the lifecycle of a script is to accept that however talented or experienced a writer may be, great scripts are never completed in a first draft. Development as a process is a natural part of bringing a script to life, and writers need time to unearth thoughts and feelings about a story. It takes time for characters to emerge and plot to solidify, and writing is a constant process of revision and exploration, switching between creative and critical skills, sustained by constructive feedback and discussion.

Common pitfalls of development are that writers become bored with the project, they begin to doubt the story or their ability to write it, they forget why they wanted to write it in the first place, or jump ship to new ideas simply because they feel fresher. First drafts are often loose and too long and need to be trimmed and tightened, but can have great energy, whereas later drafts are sometimes more mechanically effective but in danger of losing the spark. Screenwriters need to be aware of potential problems and remind themselves of the process and its natural cycle. Writers can also get very close to their stories and find it difficult to see which areas need work. This is why the script editor plays an essential part in any screenplay, and writers need to embrace and work effectively with feedback as this will improve development hugely and result in stronger, tighter, more polished scripts. Creative ways of working with feedback are offered in Chapters 6 and 8.

Script to screen

Since the screenwriter does not deliver a final piece of work but only the map towards the film or TV drama, it is essential for screenwriters to have a solid understanding of the life of a screenplay not only during its writing but of the midwifery into its final form. It is an enlightening practice for budding screenwriters to offer short scripts for production, however low budget, to experience the reality of letting go of material and gain a sense of what works on screen as opposed to on the page. It is also important to have an overview of how commission works; screenwriters are often asked to make changes based on practical, financial reasons, and a successful screenwriting career does not only depend on talent but the ability to work with others within the confinements of the form.

Most production companies or funding bodies employ script readers to sift through the vast piles of material they are sent each week. Novice writers can gain a huge amount of insight into the development process by seeking employment as readers, where they will be party to the commissioning process and how development decisions are made (see Chapter 6). Whatever type of story a writer wishes to sell, it is never simply a question of whether it is well written but also if it works for its intended audience and can find a way into the heart of financiers. The writing of a script includes two different parts of the process and it is crucial for a screenwriter to pay attention to both: first, the relationship between writer and script (personal reasons for writing the script) and second, the communication of that script to its intended audience (ensuring the script is made). Some writers are more concerned with their own relationship to the story (what they want to express) than with considering how to best build the bridge between story and audience (how it will be received) but this is not enough. It is the responsibility of every screenwriter to not only hone their writerly craft, but keep up to date with the current state of affairs in the industry and gain a solid grasp of how and why scripts sell, and how distribution, marketing and sales impact upon scripts. Regularly reading industry journals such as *Broadcast* and *Screen International* is not only useful, but essential.

Working with genre

Most screenwriting books deal with the concept of genre as a separate entity, something which works alongside story, structure and character and can be added or applied during some stage of development. What we propose in this book is different. We would like to argue that genre cannot be studied alone, as it deeply informs every element of screen-writing. Rather than developing a story and then assigning it a genre, we believe story comes out of genre. The same applies to character. Rather than identifying generic characters in, say, a thriller and then apply-ing them where appropriate, the thriller film requires a set of charac-ters which are integral to the working of the narrative. If these types (vulnerable victim, crazed killer, cop) did not exist in the first place, driving the story forward in a particularly structured way, then what was being written would not be a thriller but something else. Genre cannot be forced upon a project; it must emanate from it, encapsulat-ing all that it is and all that the audience will understand it as. Genre will thus be discussed as a *tool* which can be used to shape the vari-ous elements of screenwriting discussed: idea and character, structure, visual storytelling and dialogue. This is a somewhat novel approach to the understanding of genre, but one we think will foster a better grasp of the concept and which develops creativity and critical awareness as opposed to marketability, rigidity and commercial constraint. Chapter 6 will discuss the cultures surrounding screenwriting genre, detailing its industrial and critical contexts as well as offering specific tools for working with genre. Chapter 13 will then revisit genre to consider it in speculative form.

2 Subject: Ideas into Character

Writing a successful screenplay is not just dependent upon excellent craft, but the suitability and desirability of the idea. There are a number of issues to address at an early stage of development, long before any writing of the script. Screenwriters must ask themselves, what makes an idea suitable for the screen? What is its essence? How does the idea transform into fully fledged story? What criteria should be used when deciding which idea to develop? Such questions will help writers create and select strong ideas that fit the medium, be it feature film, television or shorts.

At an even earlier stage, work needs to be done to flex the creative muscles and allow the flow of ideas to start. Unfortunately, this is a much-overlooked aspect of screenwriting, and unlike novelists or poets, novice screenwriters tend to have little sense of the practice of having ideas. Rather than an innate talent, we would argue that creative skills can be taught and improved; a crucial part of any screenwriter's toolkit. This is discussed in Chapter 9, with accompanying exercises in Chapter 14.

Once an idea has been birthed and chosen, the next step is to ensure its seed holds enough power for a full script to blossom forth. A quick, effective way of testing ideas is by exploring story architecture through pitching or sequence outlines (see Chapters 1, 3 and 9). This allows writers to get a feel for whether an idea is worth spending time on, without having to go to script. Most of all, in order to make choices about what story to tell, it is essential to possess a good understanding of the building blocks that make-up narrative and make screenwriting stories unique.

What is a story?

In screenwriting contexts, story is often discussed in terms of conflict. Conflict is seen as the lifeblood of drama, providing obstacles to the character journey. Making the journey difficult for a character creates the need for action, and provides evidence for the audience of how important the goal is, since the actions taken (the type of action, and what lengths a character is willing to go to) show to what degree the character desires the goal, providing a sense of what is at stake should the character fail to achieve their objective. Conflict thus serves a double purpose, as it creates both action and a demonstration of commitment. However, pure conflict unconnected to theme or character arc can easily become a series of empty actions, so conflict in itself does not necessarily create story; it creates a series of events. What narrative requires is *meaningful* conflict, moving the character in the direction they need to go, both *physically* and *emotionally*. This is what the *character objective* provides. Without understanding what a character wants, there is no sense of what obstacle would best stand in their way, and help them develop the emotional spine that finds its expression in the resolution. Claudia Hunter-Johnson refers to this as the need to connect: 'The conflict and surface events are like waves, but underneath is an emotional tide – the ebb and flow of human connection. It's just as essential to story as conflict but it has been essentially overlooked' (2000: 3).

A story thus needs both a main *objective* and relevant *obstacles* to define and develop this objective. Conflict should be meaningful and relevant not only in terms of world, tone, genre and plot, but also in how obstacles challenge the character to develop in the way the story arc, theme and subtext requires. In this way, *story can be seen as a series of chain reactions produced by conflict but directed by objective*. An action causes a reaction and a decision to produce further action, which in turn gives rise to new problems, series of actions and attempted solutions. A formula for screenplay narrative could thus be:

Obstacle + Objective = Reaction → Decision → Action

Seeing the narrative as a series of events not only built around action but also reaction and decision, results in screenplays which pay attention to the inner life of characters and their developing emotions instead of focusing solely on outer actions. By creating such moments, the story cuts deeper and emotion is externalised in more effective ways. This is discussed further in Chapter 3 in relation to scene structure and Chapter 4 with regards to visual storytelling.

Character and plot

Character and plot are often pitted against one another in screenwriting terms, and expressions such as *character driven* and *plot driven* suggest a screenplay may be one or the other. Instead, we argue that both character and plot are equally important because they are inherently interdependent. Plot – a sequence of events – is devised to bring about a character's development; character – agent of the story – only develops because he or she undertakes the plot. In reality a drama cannot be plot driven because it is the character that drives the narrative. It is the character who possesses the dramatic need, undertakes the challenge and faces the journey of overcoming obstacles (see Chapter 3), so it is the character that moves the story forward. The plot is the result of the character's drive, the situations and experiences that come out of their choices. Some genres such as action adventure place heavy emphasis on plot, but are at heart still driven by protagonists and antagonists who battle each other for power; character driven with weight on the physical plot (chases, fights, explosions). As characters make a choice which results in action, character is plot; since plot is the result of character choice, plot is character.

Robert McKee uses the terms *character* and *structure* to make a similar point. For him, the true nature of character is revealed by the choices made and acted out, creating dramatic structure: 'As he chooses, he is' (1999: 101). His definitions of structure and character are:

> The function of STRUCTURE is to provide progressively building pressures that force characters into more and more difficult dilemmas where they must make more and more difficult risk-taking choices and actions, gradually revealing their true natures, even down to the unconscious self.
>
> The function of CHARACTER is to bring to the story the qualities of characterization necessary to convincingly act out choices. Put simply, a character must be credible: young enough or old enough, strong or weak, worldly or naïve, educated or ignorant, generous or selfish, witty or dull, in the right proportions.
>
> (Ibid.: 105–6)

These summaries mark the symbiotic relationship of character and plot, which work with and for each other to create coherent and satisfying narratives. Ideas of structure will be developed extensively in the following chapter, but it is important to note here that character is an integral part of it. Many screenwriting books deal with character creation on a surface level, suggesting ways to develop screen persona. Although these can be useful – character physicality, personality and voice – what needs to be addressed first and foremost is their inner make-up. This has the most impact upon story and structure, and so character psychology and issues related to character drive should be explored fully in early stages of development. Screenwriters should always remind themselves of the close relationship between character (emotion) and plot (physical action):

> Structure and character are interlocked. The event structure of a story is created out of the choices that characters make under pressure and the actions they choose to take, while characters are the creatures who are revealed and changed by how they choose to act under pressure. If you change one, you change the other.
>
> (Ibid.: 106)

Character journey as story

The central character journey is the essence of story, with plot and character driving the narrative forward while deepening theme and subtext. Building story from character results in solid, focused scripts and by asking specific power questions of each key character, essential information is quickly assembled which naturally creates dramatic options and direction. This is shaped and developed by the creation of central obstacles, and through these two elements a story almost builds itself. In this method, story is constructed through a set of character responses to *action, reaction* and *decision*, the chain of which results in naturally progressing the narrative. The character arc created by interplay between objective and obstacle becomes the core essence of the story.

For instance, in *Muriel's Wedding*, Muriel's character want is to get married – even the title says so – but her need is to realise that friendship with Rhonda is more important. Both the want and need is related to Muriel's sense of self-worth, and as Rhonda helps her value herself, Muriel realises she does not need to get married to prove her worth to the false friends she tried to fit in with.

In *Cocoon*, the main characters share the same objective – to be young and full of life. By employing a protagonist *trio*, different characters enable different attitudes to the story problem, leading to thematic depth and credibility. In the end they get what they want but in a manner they could not have imagined. Here, the want and need remain closely linked; throughout the story the want remains the same (to be filled with life force) but the *context* for the want changes, as they gain a greater appreciation for life, becoming able to enter immortality (symbolic death). Their want is to live, their need is to learn to live.

Thus, when they get what they want, they are able to receive it, having matured emotionally.

In *Wonder Boys*, the protagonist's objective is stated clearly early on, although he himself cannot articulate it. As Grady Tripp's lover Sarah reveals she is pregnant, they consider this problem in silent agony. In desperation and irony, she suggests they could divorce their spouses, get married and have the baby. This seems impossible, yet signals a clear statement of intent. Grady spends the rest of the film trying to reach the place where he can accept this is his want. Once he realises it, things fall into place quickly, and so it is his emotional journey to accepting his love for Sarah that is the story, as opposed to a physical journey of divorce, marriage and birth. It is because of this that the protagonist objective is stated by Sarah rather than by Grady, as he is at this point unable to express it. Through the physical journey of helping student James, Grady is able to release himself from the hell he has created – not only from his current marriage but since James' novel will help editor Crabtree succeed, Grady can stop his obsessive and unproductive writing, becoming free as his pages scatter to the wind. The physical plot – getting to know James and dealing with his writing problem – leads Grady to the point where he can finally admit that what he wants is life with Sarah and the baby.

Power questions, used by many screenwriting theorists in various forms but particularly championed by Laurie Hutzler's *Character Maps* (www.emotionaltoolbox.com), get to the crucial heart of drama within a character. We would set them out as follows:

- What does s/he *want*?
- What does s/he *need*?
- What does s/he *dream* of?
- What does s/he *fear*?
- What is his/her main *strength*?
- What is his/her main *weakness*?
- What is his/her main *problem*?

These questions access the areas within a character that hold most dramatic and thematic tension, the places with the highest stakes and deepest resonances, and when information from various characters is combined, powerful relationships, turning points and character journeys quickly emerge.

Knowing what questions to ask of characters thus serves as a key that naturally opens the door to plot, as long as theme remains clear.

To construct a cohesive script, all story strands have to weave together with thematic focus. During development, there are a hundred different choices at every turn, so writers needs to know how to opt for the right ones. By using a *narrative compass* stated in clear, simple language, writers can ensure all creative decisions serve the same dramatic purpose. One way to articulate this 'compass' is through the common concept of *central dramatic question* (CDQ). The CDQ is what makes the audience want to know what will happen next. Although, as will be seen in Chapter 3, each act and sequence has its own dramatic question, the CDQ is the issue which runs throughout the whole narrative. It often relates to surface plot rather than theme, though this depends on the genre. In *Misery*, the CDQ could be 'will Paul escape his number one fan and survive?'; in *Muriel's Wedding*, 'will Muriel get married?'; and in *Tillsammans*, 'will they find a way of living together?'

Another method of evolving plot from character is to explore back-stories. However, general questions regarding school, family life and hobbies only scratch the surface; they can be useful, but do not often ignite plot ideas. Instead, it is more effective to find the *relevant focus* to backstory questions, by understanding what the central conflict or connection is between characters. For instance, if the story is about Linval wanting to prove himself a master mathematician in order to find his worth in society, relevant questions may be: how he first got interested in maths, what numbers mean to him, how becoming maths-mad affects other areas of his life, how he felt included or excluded in family and school, what he is ashamed of and proud of in himself, what spurs him on in difficult moments. Such questions feed directly into the dramatic territory and character arc to inspire plot and story ideas. Note that exploring character in this way is not restricted to a notion of backstory as distant *past*, but also *present* day attitudes. It is these basic *attitudes* that make up a character and reveal their complex and rich personas. Chapter 7 offers a number of exercises on this subject.

The role of the protagonist

In classical narrative, the story is based around one central character. The protagonist serves as a link between story and audience, the eyes through which the audience experiences the story. It is not only a link for information, however, but an essential connection where the audience is invited to identify with the protagonist and through this care about what happens in the story. Hence, traditionally protagonists were required to be sympathetic. These days, it is more common to discuss protagonists as empathetic, not necessarily likeable but definitely interesting and engaging. There are several films with 'difficult' central characters (so-called anti-heroes) such as *Man Bites Dog*, *Groundhog Day* and *Fight Club*. Such films usually find something that brings the audience onto their side, whether a moment of pain (physical or emotional), seeing them with someone who is even worse, or having a charming humour or quick intelligence.

Who the central character will be depends on the type of audience the writer wants to attract. Occasionally writers do not pick the right protagonist, either by not creating a strong enough character to carry the narrative or by misunderstanding character functions. Conventionally the protagonist is the character travelling the longest journey (emotionally), undergoes the biggest change or faces the biggest problem. This is a useful place to start when analysing a story to see if it has found its proper protagonist, but it is also important to remember these are *guidelines* not *rules*, and there are exceptions which work well, depending on style, genre and dramatic approach.

In *Muriel's Wedding*, Muriel Heslop is clearly the protagonist. She changes dramatically, from pathetic shoplifter to confident adult, able to leave adolescence behind, but as an independent woman instead of a wife. She may not have the biggest problem, as finding a husband seems minor in comparison with Rhonda learning to live with cancer, but even though Rhonda's physical circumstances may change the most, she is not such a different person, whereas Muriel blossoms into herself. She thus serves as the protagonist since it is the *emotional* journey which matters.

In *Fargo*, Jerry Lundegaard seems the clear protagonist during the first act. However, in the second act, police chief Marge Gunderson increasingly takes over. So who is the main character? The story certainly seems to hold Jerry at its core, a tragic figure who is the driving force behind the crime and to begin with holds the audience's sympathy. Although he is the centre of the plot, an everyday man caught in a hellish trap of his own making, the horrific results of his misconceived actions make it difficult for him to stay the primary protagonist. It is after the murders take place – after Jerry's actions stop being pathetic and turn dark – that Marge enters the narrative. She becomes the moral centre to a world where all is crumbling chaos and makes the story emotionally palatable. In this way, the audience can follow Jerry's tragic tale without too much discomfort, and as Jerry becomes increasingly desperate (his behaviour increasingly unacceptable), Marge takes over as emotional anchor, until the end, where the audience's loyalty is almost completely to her. In this way Marge becomes a mediator between audience and Jerry, the buffer that allows his story to be told. Although they share the protagonist function, both have their own objective and arc, becoming each other's antagonist – Jerry is the perpetrator of the crime Marge seeks to solve; Marge is the spoke in the wheel to Jerry's plan. Their wants are diametrically opposed: Jerry wants a crime to be committed so he can gain money for the desperate straits he has got himself into (only vaguely alluded to), and Marge wants to solve the crime and restore order. It is unusual but effective that two protagonists share the story in this way, but in so doing, *Fargo* demonstrates the value in applying guidelines to the needs of a story instead of sticking rigidly to rules.

The role of the antagonist

An antagonist is a key character providing the most difficult or important obstacle to the protagonist's objective. Often this conflict is centralised in one character, but can also exist as a series of antagonists or smaller obstacles. Conflict is created in three arenas: *other people*, *environment* (physical or ideological) and *self*.

For example, if Harold wants a dog, potential obstacles to this could be:

(1) His parents or landlord will not allow him to keep a dog (*other people*).
(2) The country he lives in does not have dogs (*physical environment*) or sees the keeping of dogs as illegal or morally unacceptable (*ideology*).
(3) He cannot afford to buy a dog, is allergic, or frightened of dogs (*self*).

Brainstorming a list of forty or fifty possible obstacles to the central protagonist objective is a very useful way to allow story to emerge from idea. From this list the writer can see if a particular theme emerges, or if a series of obstacles can be connected to create a chain of rising action. Brainstorming obstacles can be done at any time during the writing process, as long as it is viewed within context of what makes conflict relevant or meaningful.

The antagonist often shares the same objective ('want') as the protagonist, as this puts them in direct conflict with each other. It is also important to address the degree to which the antagonist desires the goal, and whether this is on equal terms with the protagonist. Will they fight as hard for the same thing? If one is likely to give up before the other, it can diffuse the central drive of the plot. On a deeper thematic level, the antagonist is also in some sense required to be 'worthy' of the protagonist, to share some qualities or values, in order for the central dramatic battle to be played out in a satisfying manner. Indeed, another approach to the antagonist function is that they *help* the protagonist fulfil their goal. They provide the obstacles that force the protagonist to take action and consider choices, evolving them from who they are at the beginning to who they become at the end. In this sense, the antagonist is a key ingredient in the protagonist's character journey and it is essential to choose the right antagonist as the conflict which naturally arises between them will steer the narrative in a particular direction.

As an action adventure, *X-Men* features a double plot structure with two sets of antagonists. Runaways Rogue and Logan (Wolverine) provide personal journeys of change. Their main antagonist is Magneto, who wants Rogue (and seemingly Logan) for his mutation machine. Xavier and Magneto provide a more thematic strand, with static opposing positions to the central dramatic problem – Xavier wants peace, Magneto wants war. Here, the main antagonist driving the narrative is Senator Kelly, representing humans, who fear mutants and want to declare war on them. Though Magneto is of course also antagonist to Xavier (and a worthy equal), Kelly is the one creating the key conflict and dramatic problem.

In *Cocoon* there is no clear antagonist, but rather a series of antagonists – the aliens, Bernie, Ben's daughter, the police. Since the aliens and old people share the same arc – to learn to appreciate life by facing death – they become friends during the second act, and so the third act needs a new antagonist, provided by Ben's daughter and the police. The police chase provides the plot pressure needed for a climax sequence, but it is the hardest choice of whether Ben should take or leave his grandson that offers thematic and emotional resonance.

Considering who is the right antagonist(s) for a story is not always straightforward nevertheless a crucial task, as the character pairing of protagonist and antagonist is what ignites the blue touch paper of plot once the right thematic combination is found.

The minor character

The idea of the *minor character* has escaped a thorough investigation from screenwriting theorists so far. Linda Seger (1990), Andrew Horton

(1999) and Rib Davis (2001) have touched upon the concept, suggesting some ways of understanding and writing them, but we suggest they can have an influential function in story design. Worthy of careful development, we propose minor characters can serve four purposes within a screenplay: to *instigate, illuminate, imitate* and *innovate*.

Instigate

The minor character can play a literal part in shaping plot, acting as someone with the potential to move the story on, shift or divert emphasis, or function to push/pull the protagonist on their journey. Horton talks about 'messengers, mediators or muddlers' (1999: 56), meaning that they can be characters who literally appear to manipulate the plot for a specific dramatic purpose. A useful example is Alec Baldwin's character Blake in *Glengarry, Glen Ross*. He appears for only one scene – seven minutes in length – but has an important function in directing the story. Having been sent by real estate gurus Mitch and Murray to the ailing Consolidated Properties office, he reduces the salesmen to a feeling of worthlessness, telling them in no uncertain terms to improve their work or be fired. He shows off his expensive watch, brags about his top of the range car and tells the salesmen he is a better man than all of them. His tone is oppressive yet inspirational, his dialogue cutting and sharp. His presence is such that he defines the rest of the story; he *is* the inciting incident, disturbing normality and giving the salesmen both a want and a need for their future action. He also sets-up the introduction of the 'Glengarry leads', a magical reward acting as bait to the salesmen, another integral moment later paid-off when they are stolen. Blake is a minor character who has *instigated* the whole story from his short but significant appearance. In detective dramas, the minor character may come in the form of someone who provides vital clues (or red herrings), paving the way for the detective's success, guiding him to the inevitable revelation of truth. The minor character may also take the form of an obstacle for a hero to overcome; the gate-keeper, the henchman, the holder of vital information. The character as obstacle tests the hero and adds to their eventual development/arc; an *instigator* of change.

Illuminate

Another function can be to illuminate the protagonist or main characters. What the minor character is or is not can help define how the audience perceives more important characters. One way in which this works is the *role* both characters take. For example, a successful manager needs people working under her to define this superior role. The ways minor characters react and interact with her tell us who she is – are they happy and look up to their leader or do they grumble and think she is an autocrat; is she hopeless at her job and usurped by a troublesome minor character? Similarly, if a protagonist is to be portrayed as a bad mother she will need children (or other mothers) to show this. They may be naughty at school and show disrespect to those in authority, or could show signs of wanting to break free from their bleak life. Either way, children as minor characters are necessary to define the role of the mother. *Personality* is another trait minor characters can help to illuminate. How they live their lives, act and even look can operate as a stark contrast to the protagonist; seeing one enables the other to be fully appreciated. Another common technique is a protagonist being portrayed by what others say and feel about them. Here a minor character can come in useful, providing vital information in chorus-like fashion for an audience about how the main character should be perceived.

Imitate

Small personalities and minor acts can be further used to *imitate* or mirror what is going on thematically. Chapter 4 explores how postmodernist themes are expressed in *Lost in Translation*, and the use of minor characters is one technique. There is the 'hooker' who comes to Bob's room, epitomising 'all things unreal' and play-acting a role to try and arouse him; the youths in the games arcade, appearing in only a shot or two, but alluding to the film's central theme; Kelly, the so-called actress, checking into the hotel using a pseudonym, constantly mistaking things and living her life through surface images. Small moments and small characters, but used to subtextually convey the film's theme and enrich the audience experience. While a screenwriter has to be careful not to be blatant, carefully constructed minor characters can amplify the theme of a story. Minor characters can also be used as 'symbols' or 'motifs' of the genre, reflecting what the writer is trying to achieve with style and audience expectation. In a horror it would be acceptable to have small characters with visible disfigurements, menacing voices, shady eyes, unexplainable movements. Certain comedies would easily accommodate teachers with wacky one-liners, cinema attendants with Tourette's and lifeguards wearing chicken suits. These are extreme examples, but suggest that whatever the genre, minor characters can be inserted to reinforce style and theme, and can be seen as a way of *imitating* what is going on beneath the surface.

Innovate

Screenplay innovation is where minor characters can come into their own and make writing distinctive. They can be a way of making the story *the writer's own*, creating original and authentic style. If writers tell stories that hold universal concerns at their heart, and the way of making these stories unique is their means of expression, then the use of minor characters is a sure way of achieving this. Such characters *innovate* story. They add colour and texture to the screenplay, enabling it to entertain, enliven, relieve and refresh an audience. Often memorable screenplays are ones that display a varied and interesting palette of minor characters and *Drop Dead Gorgeous* uses this idea to the full. The ensemble of minor characters lies at the heart of the film's success; its lethal weapon: the old, overweight, chain-smoking choreographer tasked with training the beauty pageant hopefuls; last year's pageant queen now hooked-up to a drip in the hospital's bulimia wing; an older former pageant queen working in a slaughter house; the 'retarded' brother of one of the judges, who delights in stealing candy from children and making inappropriate comments; another pageant judge, who lurks around 'the girls' with a camcorder and a range of bad excuses. The film displays a rich tapestry of colourful minor characters who are defined by what they wear, do, eat, drink and say. Well defined and diverse minor characters will not only appeal to the audience but will add much needed visual and aural pace to the screenplay. The trick is to give the audience minor characters they want to see more of; make them hungry for their screen presence, and when they are used, make sure what they do and say is perfect. It is counterproductive having an innovative minor character who just ambles through a scene. They need credentials; they may have a visual quirk, or a unique catchphrase. Whatever the decision, it needs to be striking. The minor character can really specify and define a script; use them to *innovate* the work.

3 Structure and Narrative

It is not only *content* that creates meaning (what is in a scene) but also its *form* (how scenes relate to one another). Structure is one of the most important storytelling tools, as it creates pace, rhythm, atmosphere, narrative flow, point of view, a context for meaning and a fundamental way to interweave subtext. Structure makes story cohesive but, as with character and theme, it is often most successful when unearthed, rather than blindly applied like a prefab formula. Sophisticated scripts also use the concept of *deep structure*, where rhythm and form reflect the theme.

Physical and emotional journeys

Screenplays do not work solely on a literal, external level but on a deeper, internalised level where characters learn lessons and grow. The external journey undertaken can be seen as somewhat secondary to the importance of the internal journey experienced. This idea ties together with narrative pleasure (discussed in Chapter 10), but for now it is important to clarify distinctions between these two 'DNA strands' of structure.

Linda Aronson writes about the dual nature of narrative within a screenplay, identifying the importance that the external and internal threads have upon the story and the way they work together (2001: 51–104). She acknowledges commonly used terms in screenwriting parlance, such as *main plot* and *foreground story* for the plot-driven strand and *subplot* and *background story* for the character-driven, but decides to devise her own terms: *action line* and *relationship line*. Although action line captures the essence of what that part of the story is about, that is, characters doing things and acting-out choices, the term may be loaded with signification to action-based and plot-heavy movies. Similarly, relationship line could have connotations with love and romance, and although many films operate on some romantic level, it is not always the case that this part of the story is what is meant by the relationship line. Therefore, we propose that more useful terms to use are *physical journey* and *emotional journey*. Physical may be more appropriate than action because it is not suggestive of an action-based character in hard pursuit of their goal. Physical is inclusive of different genres and styles of film, still encompassing the strand of the narrative which is a literal, external pursuit: the physical journey to cross the desert, the physical act of finding the killer, the physical fight for survival. Emotional journey is inclusive of films whose concerns are with mental and abstract journeys as well as romantic: the emotional journey to happiness, the emotional development of trust, the emotional catharsis of relinquishing guilt. Considering the differences between story and plot, we see that plot can represent the physical journey as it is an externalised version of the emotional journey – the story – taking place within.

Aronson argues that 'in many films the main plot or action line only exists to permit the relationship line ... to happen' (Ibid.: 54), highlighting that whatever physical battle goes on, it is really emotional development that strikes the biggest chord with an audience. We would question the use of the word 'only.' It may be that the true nature of the drama, the story, is what is going on emotionally, but the fact that the events are structured in such a way to bring about this emotional journey cannot be ignored or seen as secondary. For a character to experience an emotional arc, he usually encounters and overcomes a series of obstacles testing his inner strengths and abilities. Therefore, although dramatic events can be seen as a primary device to guide the emotional journey, the events themselves can be seen as an extension of character and emotion in that they are the result of choices made by the character. Robert McKee's thoughts are useful here: 'structure *is* character. Character *is* structure' (1999: 100). Both physical and emotional journeys work in a symbiotic relationship, reliant upon each other to push and pull the character through the narrative. As physical and emotional journeys progress, the increased energy of the two brings them to a mutual climax which is often found in the same or closely related event (Aronson, 2001: 57). Sometimes known as the *obligatory scene*, this is an event the narrative has been leading to and the audience waiting for, a moment of relief where something desperately required by the story finally occurs. It can be the final uniting of a troubled couple, the re-establishment of order after a major disaster, or someone finally knocking out the bad guy for good. In 'all's well that ends well', the physical and emotional journeys come to an end and resolve one another's problem.

Classical three act structure

Much has been written about classical three act structure and it is often referred to as the main aspect of screenwriting (e.g. Field, 2003; Moritz,

2001). Essentially, the basic approach to story within this template is as beginning, middle and end. If a story is an attempt to solve a problem, the beginning is the set up of that problem, the middle is the ongoing and evolving complications as a solution is sought, and the end is the resolution where the problem is either solved or the character changes their attitude towards it.

By learning how to work with tools such as act outlines, sequence outlines and step outlines, writers can speed up their development process and make it more effective, testing ideas and identifying potential problems at an early stage. This is a professional way of working that can help writers become creative and productive, and though many writers complain about feeling restricted by three act structure, a solid grasp of classical narrative is in fact a good ally to an effective working practice.

Structural architecture

Working with key required story moments – sometimes called *tent poles* – is similar to a sequence outline, but briefer. It can be the first document a writer creates, or used later to clarify structure if much has changed. The first step towards a sequence outline, it is a powerful way to identify the main turning points in a character arc:

- Status Quo
- Inciting Incident/Catalyst
- End of Act 1 Turning Point
- Act 2 Midpoint
- End of Act 2 Turning Point
- 'Hardest Choice'
- Climax/Final 'Battle'
- Resolution and End

Each tent pole moment requires only a line or two, considering both event and emotion. These become the basic structure on which the writer begins to erect the narrative, knowing that they will hold up and support the story and stop it from collapsing.

Example: *There's Something About Mary*

Status Quo – Ted has never been able to love anyone since Mary. He is miserable and needs help.

Inciting Incident – Ted's friend Dom suggests he use private detective Pat Healy to find out what Mary is like now (fulfilling his own psychopathic need to find her).

End of Act 1 – While investigating, Pat falls for Mary and, wanting her for himself, puts Ted off by trying to make her seem ludicrously unattractive. Ted still wants her (proving himself a good guy) and when old friend Bob tells him she is still single and 'a fox', he decides to go to Miami to find her.

Act 2 Midpoint – The first half of Act 2 consists mainly of Pat trying to woo Mary, and the audience discovering what kind of man Mary wants and needs. Ted has an eventful journey to Miami and is almost tried for murder, which buys Healy time before Ted arrives (the midpoint).

End of Act 2 – Ted and Mary rekindle their relationship much to the horror of Pat and Tucker/Norm. They become very close until Mary receives an anonymous letter telling the truth about Ted, making him seem yet another stalker. She rejects him and it seems impossible for Mary and Ted to be together.

'Hardest Choice' – Realising that Mary and Brett's potential marriage was sabotaged by Tucker/Norm, Ted decides to reunite them, giving up any possibility of having Mary for himself.

Climax/Final 'Battle' – The truth of Mary's crazy admirers is revealed. They gather round, insisting she choose one, 'battling' over her until Ted arrives with Brett, who seemingly becomes the 'winner'.

Resolution – Ted walks away, his dream in tatters. Mary runs after him, realising he is the one for her. They kiss.

Based on the tent pole list, the sequence outline allows writers achieve a quick overview of the narrative and is a powerful tool in checking structure. It offers slightly more in terms of how each major sequence links together and how character arcs progress through the narrative. Nearly all feature scripts can be divided into eight sequences: two in Act 1, four in Act 2 (two before and two after the midpoint), and two in Act 3. Most sequences end after a major *turning point*, moments where something so substantial happens that things have to change, a decision or commitment that creates a new question or plan of action, truly raising the stakes. Often made up of two beats (decision and action), the turning point always ties into the bigger, overall dramatic question.

As suggested by Howard (2004) and Gulino (2004), a common formulation of the sequence narrative pattern is as follows:

Sequence 1 sets up world and the status quo/problem of the protagonist's life, leading into the inciting incident, the event that causes disturbance of the status quo and forces the story into motion (the 'why now' question).

Sequence 2 sees the protagonist struggle with the new problem, leading to a decision to deal with it. This turning point becomes the end of Act 1.

In **Sequence 3** the protagonist tries to solve the problem with a *plan of action*, doing what seems easiest first (rising action). Often more effort is needed as the problem does not go away.

In **Sequence 4** the protagonist tries harder, or applies more serious tactics. Obstacles get bigger, requiring more effort, and stakes are raised. The midpoint – a 'spoke in the wheel' of their plan – usually comes here, spinning the action into a new direction.

During **Sequence 5** the protagonist reacts to and acts upon the midpoint change. Often they are re-inspired with a new plan; same objective, different action. Subplots can become important, depending on genre needs.

Though working hard, **Sequence 6** shows the protagonist as still unsuccessful, culminating in the end-of-act-two decision. In a story with a happy ending, this is usually the 'lowest point' (hopelessness), furthest away from the goal. In a tragedy, things seem hopeful at last. This creates space for the maximum amount of drama in the third act.

Sequence 7 sees the climax or the biggest battle, incorporating the 'hardest choice' for the protagonist. Often there is a false resolution and sometimes a twist or unexpected event.

Sequence 8 is the resolution proper, both of plot and theme. This can also be the climax scene, depending on story needs, and can include aftermath and epilogue, tying ends together.

It is excellent practice to regularly analyse films according to either the tent poles or sequence outline template. Structure is not set in stone, but shifts according to genre, style and the needs of individual stories, and by analysing real examples, writers gain a sense of how structure can *serve* rather than *restrict* a story. Understanding how sequences function also helps writers focus on the overall dramatic goal, and ensures they do not get lost in the second half of the screenplay (a common problem).

Example: *Misery*

ACT 1 Question: *'Will Paul get better?'*

Sequence 1 – Paul Sheldon is a writer. He finishes a new novel and celebrates in his usual way. As he leaves to go home, there is a snowstorm and he crashes the car (inciting incident). On the verge of death, he is saved by a mysterious figure.

Sequence 2 – Paul wakes to find that his saviour is Annie, a local nurse and number one fan. She says the phone lines are down but she will take him to hospital as soon as the weather improves. She looks after him and he is grateful. She asks if she can read his new book but is horrified at the bad language and forces him to burn it. He is furious and heartbroken (end of Act 1).

ACT 2 Question: *'Will Paul get away?'*

Sequence 3 – Feeling that Annie is unhinged, Paul has a new plan – to get away. He stockpiles painkillers and tries to be nice to her. But Annie also has a plan – she has read the latest *Misery* novel and forces Paul to write a new book to bring Misery back to life, the thing Paul least wants to do. She reveals nobody knows he is there, that she has lied to him and he is on his own.

Sequence 4 – Realising he is not safe, Paul tries all he can to get away. He manages to escape from his room but cannot get out of the locked house. He half-heartedly writes *Misery* but Annie is not happy; she demands a proper book. He suggests a celebratory dinner which she joyfully accepts. The climax of his plan, it comes to nothing – he tries to drug her with wine but she accidentally spills it (midpoint).

Sequence 5 – Paul has to start from scratch with a new plan (same objective, different action). To keep Annie happy, he writes the *Misery* book. He also grows stronger as his body recovers. Buster the detective keeps investigating and Paul gets out of his room a second time, finding Annie's scrapbook. He realises she is a murderer and a psychopath, creating escalating danger. She returns and realises he has been out. Determined to keep him with her, she hobbles him. This is the lowest point as he seems more unlikely than ever to achieve his objective of escaping (end of Act 2).

ACT 3 Question: *'Will Paul get away alive?'*

Sequence 6 – Paul no longer pretends to like Annie; they are open enemies, no more game playing. No more writing is shown, instead Buster cracks the case and comes to the house. Paul thinks he is saved but Annie sedates him and hides him in the cellar. Buster searches then leaves, but runs back in after hearing a crash. Paul calls out and just as we think he will be saved, Annie blasts Buster away with a shotgun. All external hope of rescue is removed.

Sequence 7 – Annie reveals her plan for a suicide pact (imminent death). Paul persuades her to let him finish the book first. She agrees and in a mirror scene to the beginning, he sets fire to *Misery* – the manuscript <u>she</u> treasures as opposed to the one she made him burn that <u>he</u> treasured. This unleashes the final *biggest battle* as they fight to the death. True to the genre, a false end occurs as Paul thinks he has killed her; but Annie takes one last stab. He finally kills her with the pig ornament (climax and plot resolution).

Sequence 8 – Back home (he has achieved his objective), Paul lunches with his agent. His 'real' book has been re-written and he is achieving the critical success he wanted (emotional arc objective). This no longer seems as important though as Paul has been scarred by the experience with Annie. He is changed and no longer wants the same thing (emotional and thematic resolution). True to genre, an 'open end' suggests danger will never quite go away as a waitress appears, she too proclaiming to be his number one fan.

Example: *X-Men*

Sequence 1 – Backstory of Magneto's Jewish background, providing both motivation and thematic thread (genocide). Rogue's mutant power is set-up as potentially dangerous. Political debate over mutants with Senator Kelly states the key dramatic question: 'are mutants dangerous?' Xavier and Magneto are old friends but now on opposite sides; Magneto the extremist who insists mutants are the future, Xavier believing there is a way for humans and mutants to live together.

Sequence 2 – Runaway Rogue encounters Wolverine in a remote bar. Discovering he is a mutant, she hitches a lift. They are both loners, pained about their powers. The vehicle crashes and Sabretooth (Magneto's henchman) battles Logan, who shows his restorative healing powers. Storm and Cyclops save them, taking them back to X-Men headquarters. End of Act 1.

Sequence 3 – Logan meets Dr Jean and Xavier. Xavier needs to find out why Magneto wants Logan and offers help for Logan to find out who and what he is (providing hope). Extensive exposition depicts the war brewing. Xavier provides an alternative viewpoint on mutants as dangerous, suggesting they can be more of a danger to themselves.

Sequence 4 – Senator Kelly is kidnapped by shape-shifting Mystique and taken to Magneto, who transforms Kelly into what he most hates and fears: a mutant (thematic arc midpoint). Back in the school, Logan is warned off Jean by Cyclops, and has troubled nightmares. He accidentally hurts Rogue, who borrows his powers to heal herself (emotional arc midpoint).

Sequence 5 – Kelly escapes from Magneto and returns to society a changed man. Mystique shape-shifts into Rogue's friend and tells her she has broken the rules and is now an outcast among the outcasts. Rogue leaves, a runaway once more. Xavier uses the Cerebro machine to find Rogue and sends Storm and Cyclops to get her. Logan disobeys orders and follows them.

Sequence 6 – Logan finds Rogue on the train; they forge a deeper bond and Logan promises to take care of her. Sabretooth and Toad battle Storm and Cyclops at the station, while Magneto enters the train – but he wants Rogue, not Logan. As he leaves, he is stopped by the police and Xavier. Clearly on different sides, Magneto wins as Xavier is not 'willing to make sacrifices' (kill for the cause). They let Magneto go, taking Rogue with them. End of Act 2.

Sequence 7 – Storm asks Logan to join them, but he is disparaging about the X-Men and agrees with Magneto that there is a war coming. Storm tells him it is time to choose sides. Senator Kelly arrives at the school needing their help, and Xavier grasps Magneto's plan, why he needs Rogue and the danger she is in. Kelly dies and they need to save Rogue (Logan's aim) and stop Magneto (Xavier's aim). When Xavier uses the Cerebro machine, he is almost killed by Mystique's sabotage, so with Xavier out of action, it is up to the younger team to save Rogue and the gathered world leaders.

Sequence 8 – Logan has become an X-Man, wearing the uniform as they go into battle (he has chosen sides). The X-Men battle Mystique, Toad and Sabretooth, killing the latter two. This clears the way for the bigger battle with Magneto. He traps them and places them in compromising situations where they cannot use their powers. Logan dares to hurt himself to help Rogue and frees himself. Logan defeats Magneto and rescues Rogue but needs the help of the others (acts as part of the team, not alone). Logan risks himself to bring Rogue back to life, offering his life force to her in a reversed mirror scene from the midpoint.

Rogue lives, Logan recovers, along with Xavier (plot resolution). A double set-up for the sequel also works as a thematic resolution: Xavier tells Logan where he might discover what happened to him, and although he leaves as a loner, Logan promises Rogue he will come back (they both know they belong). Xavier visits Magneto in his plastic prison, playing chess and debating politics, neither changing their position: Magneto insists war is coming; Xavier continues his search for hope. This is the core problem the *X-Men* franchise cannot do without, and so though Logan and Rogue develop, the thematic arc of the war has not been resolved, in order for *X-Men 2* to continue the story.

Beginnings and endings

Two particularly crucial aspects of structure, beginnings and endings bookend the story in a thematic, narrative and stylistic manner. The way they are offered can have great impact on how an audience relates to the story and 'signs their contract' with it.

Opening scenes have a heavy task load, and have to achieve it in as engaging and as strong a way as possible to make sure the audience will invest in the story and keep watching. The right opening scene depends on the type of story and genre, how much the story wants to reveal to the audience, and what needs to be saved for later. However, usually an opening scene or sequence needs to:

- Introduce the world of the story.
- Establish the rules of the world.
- Set the tone and style (audience expectations of the film).
- Establish connection between film and audience to keep them watching, usually through a dramatic hook and/or connection to character.
- Introduce a sense of the central dramatic question and theme.
- Introduce most of the main characters and their relationships.
- Introduce a sense of the protagonist's objective and main problem.

A useful element to consider is the *opening image*; the first thing the audience sees or hears of the film and how that will impact upon what is to come. Often an effective opening image (such as in *Tootsie*) gives large amounts of concentrated information about character, world and theme (opening image is often closely related to theme). In *Toy Story*, there is no such specific opening image but rather a strong *opening sequence.*

Endings can also be complex. There are multiple story strands to pay-off and resolve so the audience feels satisfied when it is over. Just as beginnings are crucial since they have to hook viewers in, endings are vital as they determine the audience's final feelings about what they have seen. If most of a script is superb but the end lets it down, an audience can feel cheated, frustrated, annoyed or cynical. The job of the ending is to deliver what has been promised in a suitable, credible way. To achieve this, writers usually have to consider the following:

- Resolving different story strands.
- The order in which the strands are resolved.
- Picking up pace and increasing tension.
- What is the most 'difficult choice' for the protagonist?
- What is the 'biggest battle' for the protagonist?
- What revelations and/or twists will be paid-off?
- Ending theme and character arc as well as plot.
- Showing how the characters' resolution affects not only them but also the world at large for a bigger emotional and moral impact.

A common problem with endings is related to resolving only physical plot and not the deeper, emotional character arc or theme. If, for example, the protagonist has found the treasure and beaten back her fiercest competitor, she might also have to finally deal with having lost faith in the world or realising she is her own worst enemy. Sometimes these moments can be part of the same beat but it is important to be clear about including both. In *Groundhog Day*, time does not only start again for Phil but he also realises what unselfish love is and how to be a better person. In *Misery*, Paul does not only escape his number one fan but has to rethink what success means to him.

One of the key considerations when writing endings is the *order* strands are resolved in, as this shows the audience what is of most significance. The most thematically significant struggle should normally be resolved last, with others working backwards in order of importance. If there are twists and surprises, it is crucial to remember the thematic or emotional end as the real punctuation to the story since this is what gives it richness and meaning. When structuring end sequences, writers need to work out the thematically preferred order and find a way to fit the plot to this rather than let plot hijack those crucial final pages.

Further discussions of issues related to structure, including narrative alternatives and an overarching concept of its purpose, are offered in Chapter 10.

Scene structure

Just as a complete story follows an arc, so does each scene within it. Strong screenwriting requires control of scenes so they are effective and powerful in a relevant manner to the script. Novice writers often make the mistake of creating overlong and loose scenes which compromise pace, subtlety and subtext, and diffuse the impact of the narrative. The right structure for a scene depends on whether it is dedicated to action, reaction or decision (or combinations of), but in classical narrative, every scene tends to be constructed around a moment of change, creating a string of plot points inferring the whole. Because of this, scene and structural work are closely related and it is difficult to achieve good scene writing without a clear sense of the overall narrative structure and its different layers of meaning. We feel it is important to discuss scene writing at length, therefore the rest of this chapter will discuss the purpose and structure of scenes, and Chapter 4 will look at specific visual storytelling techniques in scene writing.

What is a good scene?

In general there has been a lack of theory related to scene writing. Many authors focus on story structure, genre and character as the major building blocks of screenwriting. However, without solid understanding of what makes a scene work, even the most well-structured script will fail. When considering scene structure it is useful to discuss general scene writing technique and the purpose of a scene in relation to the complete narrative. The first thing to bear in mind is that a good scene has no ideal length, structure or tone. It does not necessarily have to have conflict, rising action, great dialogue or thematic subtext, though these elements generally help. Instead, *a good scene is a scene which above all knows its purpose and serves this in the most appropriate and engaging way.* This means the writer (producer, script editor and director) has to first and foremost understand (and agree) what the purpose of a particular scene is. Much scene work tends to be intuitive but it is very useful, not only for writers but all development personnel, to analyse and approach them with a committed level of craft.

Finding the purpose of a scene

Deciding the purpose of a scene is a combination of understanding structure and character (plot, story and rhythm). A well written, effective scene will almost always achieve more than one task, indeed should probably achieve at least three or four. It depends on where and when it comes in the story, what has preceded it and what follows. Often a scene has a main function, with other minor tasks attached. The purpose of a scene can be to establish character, clarify motivation, give false or true information, set-up or pay-off a situation, move plot forward, create credibility, raise or relieve tension, give a breather, or make the audience laugh or cry.

The first step to good scene writing is a good step outline, breaking the story into scenes, defining each by an 'outer' and 'inner' beat, a physical event and an emotion. By identifying the reason for a scene, the writer can see how it fits into the bigger picture. The first question to ask of any scene is: is it needed at all? Writers have to be brutally honest with their material, and if a scene is not working, or not working hard enough, the best thing is often to cut it and create one that does. Poor scene writing comes down to a scene not having enough purpose, achieving only one task, or slowing down the pace. It is worth noting here that *pace* is not the same as *speed*. Good screenwriting is about creating tight pace, but does not mean it has to fly by in a flurry of high-octane action. Sometimes a genre, style or particular story needs to be a slow 'pressure cooker', but it can still have tight pace in the sense that it contains no superfluous material in its scenes.

To sustain both pace and purpose, these central questions can be asked of each scene:

- Where does the scene come in the story?
- What is its plot point?
- What are the emotional beats?
- What is the main conflict?
- What is it really about, thematically?

Once it is established that the story does need the scene, the writer should know why, and have clarified its main purpose. After this comes the layering process of working out what else it could accomplish. For instance, the main beat might be to show the protagonist falling in love with the wrong person, but also to remind the audience she is in so much pain she is not able to see this clearly; or make the audience think it is the right person; or plant a comment that will later make the protagonist realise it is the wrong person; or up the tempo; or make sure the plot takes a new direction; or make the audience laugh.

Big scenes (not necessarily long, but structurally heavyweight) such as openings, resolutions and turning points might accomplish five, six or seven functions. This is illustrated in the analysis of the Act 1 turning point scene in *Misery* (below), which creates credibility so the plot point feels earned, builds rising action through ping-pong conflict, provides backstory, plants information that will make sense later, reveals another side to the antagonist, makes the protagonist realise his predicament, and is tense and terrifying.

Once determined what the purpose of a scene is, the writer can look at how to best let it play out on the page. Dialogue or visual description should not feature at this stage, as such details come later. For now, structure is worked with to make sure it affects the audience as necessary. As seen in the *Jaws* analysis below, a scene can move through a number of peaks and troughs, taking the audience through tension and relief, where structure and rhythm are instruments of managing emotion in the audience. As with overall story structure, scene structure is closely related to *rising action*; as the scene progresses, conflict increases and events become worse, harder, funnier, scarier. Again this is not true of all scenes, since some might have as their purpose to clear the air, give the audience a breather, or let them have a quiet moment with a character, but usually scenes begin in one place and end in another. Thus, a writer needs to ask:

- Where does the scene start emotionally?
- Where does it end emotionally?
- What has changed after this scene?
- What is the main conflict in the scene?
- What is the relationship dynamic/status/power in the scene?
- How does the relationship dynamic/status/power change as the scene progresses?

Good scene structure is about understanding and controlling the interplay between action, reaction and decision beats and orchestrating their effect on each other. Action scenes are where the main beat of the scene is an event or action, often moving the plot forward. Reaction scenes are where the main beat depicts how a character *feels* about what has happened or is about to happen. Decision scenes are where the main beat depicts a character considering taking action, weighing up options or having a realisation. A common fault is that scripts dwell more on action than reaction or decision moments, and this tends to make them less emotionally engaging. When witnessing a decision as well as an action, the audience is allowed to understand more about a character's motivation and what is at stake in making the decision, and by seeing a reaction the audience senses the moment without it having to be overtly explained.

Sometimes it is easy to think of scenes simply in terms of their plot points (action): 'Bob kills Bella', 'Bob goes to the shop', or 'Bob finds a secret formula to time travel'. But a reaction scene could be just as crucial, or more so: 'Bob despairs over having killed Bella' 'Bob gets angry as he finds the shop is shut', 'Bob is so overjoyed at discovering the secret formula he goes out to celebrate and leaves the door open, thus allowing Bella in to steal it.' Alternatively the writer can show the decision, the moment when the character decides to act but before taking the action: 'Bob deciding he can no longer let someone who stole his precious formula live', or 'deciding he has to swallow his pride and go to the only other shop in town where his ex-fiancée works with her new partner', or 'deciding it is too dangerous to know the secret of time travel so must destroy the formula (only for it to not quite have burnt out, allowing Bella to steal it and …).' The good thing about decision scenes is they are often the most tense as they make the audience wonder what the character will do; the decision suggests an action which is yet to be carried out. Such moments are therefore often ones when the audience is most involved. A scene showing whether Bob will decide to buy a pint of milk from his ex-fiancée or go home and defy his thirst can be substantially more engaging or dramatic than a scene of Bob blasting his way through an army of aliens. The choices a character makes is the mark by which the audience charts the progression and change in both character and story, and so it is crucial to witness not only the *result* of a decision (an action) but also the emotional and mental struggle that created it (the *motivation* of the action). This way a script will offer a great deal of character depth without the need for cumbersome backstory or exposition. Instead, it suggests depth by allowing the audience to spend time with the character in their most difficult moments.

Topping and tailing

Two of the most important parts of a scene are its beginning and end. In early drafts, scenes are nearly always long and loose and need a good trim, a process known as *topping and tailing*. If scenes start early and end late, they can lose energy and diffuse the meaning and impact of the moment. During the rewrite, a writer is recommended to cut as much as they can at the beginning (top) and end (tail) of each scene and find the minimum needed to make it work. Not only does this technique tighten pace, it also helps to pull viewers into the next scene. By giving the audience less and ending the scene on a narrative 'question' rather than a 'full stop', the story keeps them wanting to know what happens next. A good example is a scene early on in *Tootsie*, where Michael-as-Dorothy is about to go home from his first day on the TV soap when Julie invites him to her place to go over some lines. She will cook dinner in exchange. The audience can see how much Michael-as-Dorothy wants to accept this invitation, but also how much he knows it is not a good idea, and the scene ends on the question being asked. Instead of hearing Michael-as-Dorothy's answer and deflating the tension, the story cuts to a new scene of Michael in his flat, desperately trying to find something suitable to wear and asking his flatmate advice about what might be appropriate for a 'first date'. The audience thus receives the answer *not* in the scene the question was asked, but in the following one, pulling them through the transition. It also tightens pace by showing only the parts that are narratively needed; real-time moments of Michael-as-Dorothy replying to Julie, going home and telling his flatmate about what happened have all been cut (topped and tailed) as they are *implied* in the action. This technique allows the writer to use their precious hundred or so pages of a feature to best effect rather than waste them on the obvious and pedestrian (unless the point of a scene is to be obvious and pedestrian ...). It is worth noting that some scenes do need to get to an emotional or rhythmic 'full stop', especially if they are at the end of a sequence or act, or their function is to release tension. In such instances, the writer may find it more useful to play the scene out rather than cut it early. It all comes down to being clear about the purpose, but in general topping and tailing is a very effective tool that helps tighten a script and give it pace and power.

Scene transitions

Transitions are a crucial but often overlooked element in the anatomy of a scene. They are the unseen way each scene connects to the one before or after. A subtle tool, less about content and more about invisible structure, they are often ignored by novice writers, but can be very powerful as they allow the creation of meaning by *comparison* rather than by exposition or explanation. To understand the importance of scene transitions, consider how the scene before ended, either visually, in dialogue or emotionally. The following scene can either oppose or underscore this point, create a joke or further build tension. Transitions allow the writer great and subtle control, moving the audience from one moment to the next without spelling things out. They can also be an excellent tool in creating a rich thematic subtext, allowing the writer to show rather than tell, letting the audience join the dots themselves. This can be done through a visual motif, object or character moment. Scene transitions are all about what is *not* said, and how the audience furthers their understanding through juxtaposing moments so they become more than the sum of their parts (meaning through *comparison*), rather than by obvious explanation (meaning through *content*).

Scene structure case studies

Jaws – the midpoint scene of Quint, Hooper and Brady taking a night-time break from hunting the shark is a long scene that can be divided up into three sections: the scar sparring, the Indianapolis story and the song. Overall it is dialogue-heavy, yet holds audience attention via strategies of rising action, character conflict and tension rhythm. There is clear rising action through the scene; as the characters show off their battle scars, the injuries get gradually worse (starting off with Brody's bump on the head, then a tooth, then arms, legs, bigger shark attacks and the joke about the love affair as the biggest pain of all). Not only do the injuries increase, they also create conflict as the scene progresses, and show something at stake to engage the audience: 'who will win the sparring?' Quint, the captain who is comfortable in his environment, and Hooper, the upstart with something to prove, have been in direct conflict since they got on the boat (traditional working class vs modern upper class) but the scar scene transforms this conflict into camaraderie, Quint finally accepting Hooper into his club as someone with enough real-life experience to make him worthy. This part of the scene ends with the two of them, bare legs over one another, recognising they have shared experiences and sealing the newfound friendship with a drink.

The second part of the scene is the worst shark story of all, to top every other told earlier in the scene. The mood turns sharply from jovial to deadly serious as Quint makes his speech about going down with the Indianapolis and being left to die. The purpose of this is to remind the audience what is out there (the present threat of the shark), and what the possible fate of our heroes might be, which sets up tension of what is to come. This is why it is powerful; not because it is a long well-delivered speech about a dramatic past, but because it makes the characters (and audience) realise for the first time that this is not a game, but a matter of life and death (hence this scene as midpoint – a dramatic and crucial new understanding). During his speech Quint mentions the terror of waiting helplessly in the water, not knowing whether you are going to live or die (what the characters are doing right at this moment), and says that next time he will not wear a life jacket and be forced to wait in limbo. This comment is a plant for the end of Act 2, where Quint, realising the boat is likely to break, gets life jackets for Hooper and Brady but not one for himself. And so, with this small subtle gesture, the audience – somewhere in their subconscious – prepare for the idea of Quint as a man facing his death. The Indianapolis scene is thus the decision for the later scene which carries out the action.

The final part of this scene is the song. After Quint's story, the mood is low (realisation of death as a distinct possibility) and Quint begins to sing his 'death knell' song. Here, however, Hooper interrupts and overrides him with a more cheery (yet mournful) drinking song they all eventually join in with. The scene thus ends with the three characters bonded together, drinking, having one last moment of togetherness before the true battle begins, that is, to blow them apart. At the end, the story cuts to the shark outside, 'listening' to the song, and it is during this happy moment the mood is again sharply severed as the shark begins to attack and damage the boat. The overall structure of the scene can thus be seen to have a number of peaks and troughs, expertly guiding the audience from laughter to fear to relief to terror.

Misery – the end of Act 1 scene between Annie and Paul achieves maximum tension by a gradual development of rising action. Often, turning point scenes need to have a stronger impact than other scenes and so it is important to ensure all potential drama is capitalised upon. Here it is achieved by a constantly renegotiated battle. Annie states early on what she wants from Paul – to burn his new book. The rest of the scene sees Paul trying to avoid this and Annie having to increase pressure to get what she wants. The scene has a clear arc of conflict and objective and the audience knows what is at stake (the treasured one-off manuscript). This makes the audience want to see what will happen, the scene batting the ball from one character to the other, upping the pressure and creating the necessity of action.

In terms of the character dynamic, Paul's reactions to Annie's demands concede more and more power to her; at first he is silent, then tries to bluff her, then tries bargaining. The use of the match and matchbox is an effective visual device to show the power struggle: Annie constantly offers them to Paul but he will not accept them. As he never actually takes them, Annie literally puts them into his hands, but even then he refuses to accept defeat. Because Paul will not give Annie what she wants, she has to try harder, bringing more drama into the scene. Each tactic puts more pressure on him than the previous. At first she suggests he should do it because it is the 'right thing', then calls his bluff, then rejects his appeal to renegotiate. She does not change what she wants throughout the scene – the book must go. Her final weapon is the threat to his life and it is only when she resorts to this that she gets her way. The reason this turning point is so rich in tension is because it is a scene where both characters feel strongly about what they want – for Annie, to destroy the book, and for Paul, to save the book – and thus conflict is maximised as the battle intensifies. If Paul were to give in easily, it would not feel like a major scene; this 'ping-pong' structure of *bargaining* is what gives the scene its impact.

Another key point is the shifting in Annie's character. Much of the tension and terror in the overall story comes from Annie seeming to be an innocuous middle-aged spinster, when the truth is that she is also a psychotic obsessive monster. The audience never knows what will set her off, and throughout the film Paul (and the audience) discover more and more disturbing information about her. In this scene, Annie starts off as the 'caring nurse' (having just been dangerous and psychotic in the previous scene) and slowly derails as the scene progresses. She becomes increasingly unhinged and dangerous, talking about God's mission and revealing how truly obsessive a fan she is (she can memorise years' old interviews and knows everything about Paul), finally ending with a veiled death threat. Though understated and subtle, she is truly terrifying, and it is the first time Paul fears for his life, realising the extent of the situation he is in. Once Annie gets what she wants and Paul burns the book, however, the 'dippy Annie' returns as she trots about haplessly trying to put out the fire. This makes her instability as a character more terrifying and adds to the horror of the overall situation, contrasting a dangerous psychopath with a seemingly unthreatening fool.

A further structural point is how, right at the end of the scene, new hope arises. Paul and Annie hear a helicopter outside and for Paul this provides some sense that he might be rescued. It is important for the audience to feel some hope here (the helicopter scene is more for the audience than for the characters), to carry them into the next act and feel the balance between protagonist and antagonist is not too uneven and the struggle too hopeless. The hope that the helicopter symbolises therefore keeps the audience engaged at a crucial point when they might otherwise be lost. One tricky aspect concerning turning point scenes is that they often create rhythmical punctuation and a sense of a 'full stop', allowing the audience to breathe out. This means the story needs to work extra hard at not losing connection and pushing on into the next phase. This script does so by straight away introducing a glimmer of Paul's new plan: after the helicopter, Annie hands him pain killers and he puts them under the mattress. This will eventually become the fully formed plan that drives Paul to the midpoint of the second act.

Thematically, it is interesting to note that Annie makes Paul burn his book after he effectively 'destroys' her book (by ending the *Misery* novels). This means the cause of change for both characters is the loss of a beloved book, giving a strange balance to the relationship. It also gives Annie a narrative drive for the rest of the story, since she wants Paul to write a new *Misery* book to bring her back to life. At the climax in Act 3, Paul turns the tables on her, doing to her exactly what she does to him here; burning her valued item. The initiation to the fight to the death scene of the story's climax is Paul holding the last few pages of the new *Misery* novel and taunting Annie with them. The most important thing in the world to her, he achieves his revenge by burning them, just as she made him burn his treasured pages in this scene. There is thus a strong and satisfying symmetry in the overall story structure introduced here and fulfilled later.

4 Visual Storytelling

Screenwriting is exactly that: writing for the *screen*. This means everything that appears in a screenplay is seen or heard by the audience, and although many novice screenwriters spend much time writing dialogue, it cannot be emphasised enough that screenwriting is very much a visual medium. Of course voice is important and can be a crucial element of telling a story, but the visual importance of screenwriting needs to be appreciated fully. A common cliché, not only in screenwriting but many forms of creative and media writing, is *show, don't tell*. In this context it means writers need to carefully consider how they visually tell a story and show the audience what is happening. The narrative experience of film and television is an audio-visual one, not just audio (sound, music, dialogue), so finding ways in which story can be conveyed in pictures and imagery is vital. It is worth considering that we live in a highly visually literate culture, where people are reliant upon look and image, and can with ease understand complex and demanding ideas when portrayed visually. Screenwriters should not be afraid to allow the narrative to develop in images, using the performance space of the screenplay (the screen or, if reading, the imagination) to convey story, character, theme and meaning.

The basics of visual storytelling

Unlike novels where much of the action is imagined, or in theatre or radio where action and emotion is heard, on screen everything is seen. From a simple gesture or facial expression to more elaborate action sequences, characters inform an audience about their state of mind, feelings, wants, needs and plans by *doing*. This can be understood as *Action, Behaviour, Character* – ABC. *Action* is what an audience sees; comprised of the *behaviour* of a set of people interacting in a scene; from which *character* traits can be deduced and decisions made about a character, what they want or need, how one character views another. The observing of characters interacting in a scene has the power to tell an audience as much as, sometimes more than, the spoken word.

The skill lies in translating character – personality, emotion, descriptive adjectives – into action and behaviour.

American Beauty utilises these ideas to full effect. The film's protagonist is Lester Burnham, a middle-aged man who feels he needs a new direction in life. The opening sequence establishes the character's dramatic problem through what he does. Although it employs a voiceover crucial in creating audience identification and revealing exposition, it is the use of physical action and behaviour that promulgates a clear understanding of who Lester is. He lies lazily in bed looking at the ceiling, his face telling of the dread he fears will creep into his day. He goes to the shower and masturbates, his voice telling the audience that 'it's all downhill from here.' His pessimism for life continues as he looks out despondently from an upstairs window, watching his wife Carolyn neatly pruning the roses and talking with their neighbour. Surrounded by a suburban nightmare, Lester is running late for work. This is important because not only does it physically show us his character but it sets him apart from his wife and daughter Jane. They are waiting for him, he is the one who is late, suggesting they are more organised and in some ways 'better' than he is. Lester's own words are that he is a gigantic loser. Later in the film when Lester begins his search for a new lease of life, one of the first things he does to initiate the change is get out his old gym gear and begin to work out. This character choice to physically make a change and behave differently demonstrates the power of action and behaviour in depicting character on the screen. As screenwriters, we need to experiment with ideas around character behaviour and it is good practice to take everything known about a character and write scenes to visually depict this. These will not necessarily make it into the final draft, but develop an intrinsic awareness of how to use action and behaviour to tell an audience about character. Another useful exercise is to put a character into a given situation and see how he or she reacts. Knowing who a character is and how they usually behave, it is interesting to see how they react in a situation alien to them. For example, how would an arrogant, selfish, womanising protagonist physically react when faced with a pretty young woman wielding a knife and demanding his wallet?

The *visual grammar* of character is also important, adding an experience of story that goes beyond simple action and behaviour and is punctuated by traits such as dress and appearance, lifestyle, physical environment and gesture. These *expressers of identity* are useful tools to work with because of the function they serve in understanding story. The interplay between such elements of visual grammar and the journey being undertaken by the character can be understood by the way of *choice*: a character chooses a way of sculpting their identity through visual display. Dress and appearance can be understood as a physical space in which a character can purvey their inner self (identity) via dressing the body. This may come in the form of a character's costume: what they choose to wear on a night out, accessories they wear, or even bodily 'dressing up' such as piercings, tattoos and cosmetic surgery. If the character has to wear a particular type of dress enforced by others, it can be interesting to see how he or she may *appropriate* this outfit. Whether it is a schoolgirl who wants to glamorise her uniform or a civil servant who adds accessories to his shirt and tie, characters can appropriate what they wear to make a statement about their identity. This is very much linked to story and choice, and can be a vital way of defining character by performative visual grammar. Many of these decisions will come from the costume designer and not the writer, but it is possible (and useful) for the writer to at least consider such things because it can influence the script. If a writer knows a character would be wearing this, not wearing that, then the scene can be written to include implicit or explicit references to costume, in this way working with the scene's essential story function and colouring it with visual grammar.

Lifestyle is another feature of character through which visual expression is also possible. Factors to consider include: what does the character have on their bedroom wall? What type of newspaper or magazine do they read? What car do they drive? Where do they go on holiday? Where can they be seen eating out? Such questions, when pieced together, form a strong sense of character profile, and can reinforce the screenplay. Novice writers tend to set scenes in familiar places like kitchens, living rooms and streets, but knowing the lifestyle of a character can add texture and a sense of reality which can be played out by use of visual lifestyle depiction. This relates closely with physical environment (which will be discussed further later on). Here, the writer can use physical space and its inhabitation to suggest further profiling. For example, looking at the lifestyle questions, where does a character choose to eat out? Is it a posh restaurant or a greasy spoon? Does it have a calming and relaxed mood or is it chaotic and noisy? Although it could be said the character has no ownership of these locations – they are just places that exist – we would suggest they can be understood on a character-driven level. Firstly, the character has chosen to go to this place therefore it reveals personality and taste through physical choice. Secondly, how the character acts within and reacts to this space reveals character further; it could be a way of punctuating someone's taste, lifestyle and ability to frequent the place, or a way of juxtaposing character and space to reveal who and what this character is not. Whoever the character and whatever the physical environment, the two can work together as visual grammar to deepen the understanding of both character, and subsequently, narrative.

These techniques can be used to great effect in the opening minutes of a screenplay (see Chapter 3). Featuring as part of the 'set up' of classical narrative, the opening is often a predominantly visual sequence revealing character, story world and theme. A crucial part of the screenplay, it carefully introduces character(s) to the audience and provides essential backstory information which will help the narrative to unfold. This can quickly and effectively set up character, telling an audience who they are, what they are about, and what they want. Action, behaviour, dress, appearance, lifestyle depiction and physical environment all give an audience vital visual clues to decode in order to formulate knowledge and opinions on character.

The 'four tools technique'

Taking this grammar a step further, when considering how to realise action on the page, the *four tools* technique offers a clear working practice that quickly develops strong scene writing skills. These techniques not only develop the character-driven discussions above into story-driven ones, but offer specific practical considerations for the hands-on writing of the script. Even with the skill to think visually, translating this into actual writing on the page needs practice, and thus each tool has accompanying exercises in Chapter 7.

Specific verbs

By using verbs rather than adjectives, scene description immediately becomes more economical and punchy. Verbs are already external and dynamic and therefore innately dramatic. By choosing a verb the writer ensures the description becomes 'playable', that it will work on screen. Much of the writer's work is to ensure the story will be clear and effective on screen, and using verbs helps to approach emotional beats in an external, dramatic way rather than a nebulous internal manner. If visual storytelling is about externalising inner emotional states, using not only verbs but the technique of specific verbs accomplishes this in a simple and economic way. By being specific, a writer gives clues as to how a character is feeling, how much they want something, how important it is, or how they are reacting to what is going on. Thus, instead of saying 'she looks', a scene description might choose one of the following more evocative synonyms:

Glance, Peer, Peek, Stare, Glare, Gaze, Squint, Wink or Regard.

Each of these verbs have specific emotional connotations and encourages the audience to infer their own assumptions as to the situation, reading a character as angry, curious, shy, playful, resentful. With just one verb, the writer gives the reader maximum information about a character's internal state as well as ensuring it will play on screen.

Objects

Another effective way to show how a character feels is to give them an object to interact with. Adding objects to a scene can offer characters an opportunity to act or react (throwing it, hiding it, using it to block or distract), and can give useful clues to the status or balance of a relationship, such as who has an object, who has taken it, if there is or has been a struggle over it, if it has been stolen, if it is given away or offered, who takes it or refuses it. In this way objects quickly establish or reveal changing *dynamics* within relationships, without resorting to long-winded explanations.

Often, a script will have a few *key objects* running through the story and the way they are used in different scenes suggests not only how a character feels at that moment but how a character, relationship or situation is changing (tracking the emotional journey). In *Misery*, various book-related props such as the manuscript to Paul Sheldon's new book, the new *Misery* manuscript, the published *Misery* books, Sheldon's manuscript satchel and the typewriter are used in various ways to chart who has power over whom. By using such objects, characters can speak volumes about inner thoughts and feelings to both reader and other characters without having to spell it out in dialogue. As an object is used throughout a script, the audience/reader also begins to have certain expectations of it – how it will be used, how sought after it is, who might struggle over it – and in this way the writer can use them as *valued objects* that create tension or relief (fear and hope) and become ways to create meaning not only through action but through *comparison* and *context*.

The recurring objects in *Misery* have a symbolic and thematic resonance and coherence (books or writing paraphernalia), which makes for sophisticated storytelling, but an object does not always have to be a valued object (an object with desired status in the story). Instead, a character could be provided with an object in a scene that does not have any intrinsic value to the plot but simply works as a temporary tool to allow characters to express themselves through action, so the audience can see if they are nervous, angry, thoughtful or loving. This works in a similar way to dialogue subtext, as discussed in Chapter 5.

Environment

When writing a scene, it is essential to always consider where it is set. Even in low budget dramas, there is a lot to be said for thinking creatively around scene locations. What is the emotional beat or conflict in the scene; what do the characters want? Once established, the writer can brainstorm where to best set the scene: an open or enclosed space; private or public; a place where there is a chance of being interrupted or bringing in a third party? By setting a scene in a different location, it might also offer up new objects to be used by characters and help bring the scene alive.

Thinking back to earlier character-driven questions of visual grammar, it is useful to consider how a character feels in a location – are they comfortable or awkward, do they want to be there or get away, are they trying to hide (physically or emotionally)? In a relationship, a particular location might be better suited to one of the characters, making them feel more at ease or in control and therefore setting up a power dynamic. Locations can also add spice to a scene and make it feel fresh. It can either heighten or counterpoint the emotion in the scene and be used thematically or symbolically to create richer subtext: is a character isolated, imprisoned emotionally, lost in a crowd, overwhelmed? By putting a character in a particular environment, the writer can let one strong image speak volumes and stand back to allow the audience to find their own way to them.

Blocking and body language

Even though screenwriting is as much about reaction as action, writers often forget to write in the reactions of characters who are not talking.

Adding specific body language (e.g. 'he slumps on the chair', 'she turns away' or 'he leans against the wall, tapping his foot') can tell the reader how a character is feeling, how they are reacting to a situation and suggest what lies behind this. However, there is more to physical movement than body language. The writer may also consider how to block the scene – that is, how characters move around the location in relation to each other. When directors work with actors, they block a scene in terms of how the actor/character feels in the space as well as in relation to the camera. For writers, the camera is not their tool, but what should be considered is how characters react physically to each other and to the space. For instance, are characters facing each other? Is one standing and one sitting? Has one of them turned their back? Is one of them hanging around by the door, about to leave? Do they walk up and speak right in their face? Showing how close or distant characters are from each other can clearly show the status or changing dynamic of a relationship, or how a character feels in a space. Though this might be changed once the script is produced, the object is for the writer to create an accurate and engaging reading script that guides the reader through the emotional journey. Blocking (or staging) is one of the most effective and economic tools in a screenwriter's arsenal, and can speak volumes with just one small movement, if placed with precision and insight.

Implying the shot

The writer needs to make the reading of a script as smooth and engaging as possible. Including camera directions distances the reader from the story and takes them out of the action, forcing them to *interpret* emotion rather than *connect* to it. At this stage, the screenwriter's job is to render the emotional beats as readable as possible. Even writer–directors have to secure funding and talent and would do well in employing this approach. However, writers often think in terms of framing and camera movement, seeing the story unfold on an imaginary screen, feeling that key moments require a close up or long shot to convey meaning. Although technical directions should not be included in a script, they can be suggested by 'implying the shot'. Instead of camera direction, the writer describes what they see on their imaginary screen, *not* thinking about how it would be achieved technically, but how it looks, and writes this as the scene description. For instance, to create tension in a scene by using a close up where it cannot be seen who is there, instead of writing 'close up on hand opening door', consider 'a hand pushes down the handle and opens the door'. By writing 'hand' instead of 'the stranger opens the door' or 'Betty opens the door' the reader is automatically drawn closer into the action and 'sees' what the writer sees in their head. Or to get a sense of vastness, 'she wanders along the water's edge, a small solitary figure in a desolate landscape' is more effective than 'long shot of Lynette walking along the sea'. Writing in this manner gives a direct emotional connection to the moment, and is thus more akin to viewing the film where one receives the *effect* of a camera shot rather than having to translate and interpret what would be achieved.

Scene case studies

Strictly Ballroom – though a seemingly simple fable on the surface, this is a carefully constructed script with beautifully written details. The end scene sequence uses various excellent visual techniques to make its points in a moving, dramatic and funny way. A powerful and recurring tool is to externalise internal struggles by making them physical. The most important example is during Scott's moment of hardest choice, when he has to decide whether to dance with Liz and be part of the Federation conventions, or follow his heart and dance his own steps with Fran. This internal emotional struggle is represented by a literal physical struggle over Scott by Shirley and Doug. His mum and dad each represent a different approach to dance and as they argue and reveal to Scott the true backstory of what happened to them, they literally fight over him, pushing him back and forth, Shirley trying to push him into the arena and Doug holding him back. Furthermore, Shirley and Doug are not only a symbolic key to Scott's progression but also function as a subplot in their own right (the threat throughout is that Scott will end up like his father, with the irony being that he does but in the true manner and in so doing honours his father, heals the past and enables a happier future). Other key physical externalisations include Barry Fife finally collapsing, bringing the trophy table and his toupee tumbling down with him as the collapse of the Federation becomes undeniable, and Scott visually interrupting Barry's 'future of dance' speech by sliding onto the dance floor with Fran. By giving characters something to physically struggle over (another character, a sound cable, a dance step) the story becomes primarily told through actions and visuals.

City of God – a good example of simple but effective visual storytelling is the sequence where Bene and Thiago's relationship is sealed through a cycle race (using objects to develop a relationship). Thiago is seen to secretly break to let Bene go on and win, seeking his approval and friendship. When Bene asks Thiago to bring him cool clothes, he gives him a huge wad of cash (another object) – the seemingly most dangerous thing you could do to a drug addict, but instead this seals their friendship and shows Bene as someone who instils trust and devotion. Then Thiago gets Bene's clothes measurements by physically comparing their bodies, measuring their feet to get shoe size, the reach of their arms and backs for shirt size. The effect of this is powerful not only visually, but also emotionally. They literally (physically) become intimate at the moment their friendship is established. On a more thematic level, the scene also shows Bene 'becoming' Thiago – they are (physically) the same (size). As the purpose of the sequence is to begin Bene's transformation from Lil Ze's right-hand man to someone who wants a better life, this works as a perfect visual and thematic metaphor. Later on, this transformation is again seen physically, as Bene bleaches his hair to ginger like Thiago's and arrives at Lil Ze's wearing a loud Hawaiian shirt, proclaiming his change ('I've become a playboy'). This physical and symbolical change is what prompts the beginning of Bene's leaving of Lil Ze and hints at the possibility of the danger it might cause him. It is simple elegant moments like this that makes *City of God* far more than a string of stories woven together by voiceover narrative, as underneath the scenes themselves are constantly addressing the themes of the world and its characters.

Writing scene action

Many novice writers treat scene directions as prose, which cannot be realised in the frame and slows down reading pace. Scene action should be *written in present tense*: the character does and decides to, not did and decided to. The screenplay is an active form and living process, and the action needs to reflect this. Similarly, the writer should *only write what the audience can see*. The purpose of screen direction is to give a sense of what is unfolding within the frame, not what happened to a character twenty years ago. Of course backstory is essential and what a character is motivated by should be inferred in the story, but this should be accomplished by the actions and dialogue in the present, not stating the character's history in the middle of a scene. Overall, the style of scene action should be *tight, fluid* and *sharp*. Overly long, detailed screen directions can slow down the reading process and digress into the realms of prose fiction. Consider this:

```
SAM sits down on the wooden step. She thinks long and
hard about what has just happened, and how her life
might be from now on. She wipes a slowly dripping tear
from her pale, gaunt face, knowing that this tear will
be the first of many. After a long pause, in which she
looks around at the gloomy surroundings, she decides
to leave. She slowly manages to raise herself and walk
away, looking back at the step for one last time before
she leaves the place forever.
```

This is clearly too long and too much like prose. It slows down the reading process and takes the reader on an imaginative journey rather than one of actuality. In no way does it represent the fluidity and action of a screenplay, and for the actress playing the part, it dictates too much. Scene action might rather read like this:

```
SAM sits on the step, pensive. After a moment, a tear
rolls down her cheek.

Silence as she takes in the surroundings. Long pause.

She slowly rises and heads off, taking one last look
back. She leaves, sad.
```

Notice how the same information is presented, but in a quicker, less flowery way and how the paragraph of action is broken up. The economy of screen direction is paramount and *long screen directions should be split into smaller sections* to avoid a heavy page of text. As a general rule, *every time the dramatic beat changes, or the camera would focus on something different, a new paragraph should start*. This ensures a tight pace, and helps to formulate the page into digestible, workable parts for production.

Visual symbolism and metaphor

As well as relating to character and story, visual storytelling has the capacity to speak to audiences about wider themes and meaning; the myth of the screenplay. As well as operating locally within the story world, visual symbolism and metaphor can break out and say much more. As Charlie Moritz writes, 'developing this ability to recognise when a setting, image, or event provide both the occasion for a totally believable, engaging narrative at the surface level, as well as carrying the potential for deeper meaning is a key asset in a dramatist's armoury' (2001: 137). So, working not only on a literal level but considering the subsurface, dramas which offer a more symbolic, deeper meaning are likely to create a stronger level of identification for audiences and result in a more engaged and enriched experience.

Lost in Translation is essentially a film about two people who literally feel lost in the worlds that they inhabit. Bob and Charlotte feel like outsiders; displaced; have no direction; are being carried along by others. They crave to find meaning and hope that will help them to survive. The film can be seen as carrying an overall message of the 'postmodern' condition. It is a critique of modern society and its concerns with mass consumption, recycling messages and images, offering surface illusions, replicating reality and partaking in 'false' communication. The challenge for the protagonists is to find ways in which they can survive, even transcend, this world, finding humanity and experiencing real feelings which touch the heart. The film, therefore, must portray a world in which these characters can feel consumed and part of the mass, giving them the dreams and motivations to escape.

Bob (an actor) is driven through Tokyo city. It is bright; striking; perhaps vulgar. As he gazes somewhat amazedly out of the car window he spots on a billboard an advertisement for Suntory whisky, a product endorsed by and featuring an image of himself in a dinner suit. As well as setting up who this character is, this visual image immediately spells out the theme of consumption and the idea of someone being 'used' for capitalist means.

Settling into his hotel room, Bob receives a fax from his wife: he's forgotten his son's birthday. On a literal level this works to add to the character set-up (forgetful, distanced from family), but symbolically to reinforces the theme of postmodernism. The fax is a *copy* of something real; a means of 'false' communication. Sitting on his bed, he puts on the hotel's slippers, generating metaphorical meaning in that the character is wearing something that does not belong to him; it does not fit. That night he receives yet another fax from his wife, this time showing him different types of shelving that he can choose for his office back at home. On a symbolic level once again, these visual moments carry a deeper meaning than one solely of plot. This is a story world portrayed to the audience where nothing seems real, and truth is hard to distinguish.

In the morning Bob's hotel curtains open themselves, presumably on some sort of timer. This visually suggests he has no control over his life, being carried through by others. He goes to the bathroom and the shower fitting is too short for him, so he comically tries to squeeze under it and wash, another symbolic moment suggesting he is displaced in his current environment and is inhibited by the actions and decisions of other people.

When the audience meets Charlotte she is seen visiting a shrine, which provides a visually harsh contrast to the stifling scenes of Bob and his encounters with places and people. The audience witnesses Charlotte immersed in a succession of traditional Japanese rituals where nothing from the modern world interferes. This immediately provides a counter text to what has been seen, and begins to forge links between the characters' story worlds, their dramatic problems, and thematic statement. Charlotte later recalls this experience on the telephone, another sign of false communication, where she expresses her dissatisfaction with her current state. The earlier visual metaphors provided to the audience depict this state successfully, and the juxtaposition between nature and tradition with product and postmodernism certainly signals tensions which will be explored throughout the narrative. In the face of this admitted unhappiness, the audience sees Charlotte trying to change her appearance. She applies lipstick and alters her hair in an attempt to feel better. This has thematic importance as it reinforces notions of surface appearance, and what is *seen* is different to what actually *exists*. Looking even deeper, the difference between appearance and reality is symbolised by the fact that Charlotte's husband John is a photographer. He is often seen with a camera and goes about pursuing his photographic career, again pointing to a thematic allusion of copy and falseness.

Later, Bob is seen in his hotel room watching a repeat of a programme he was once in, where he is supposedly talking with a monkey, now dubbed in Japanese. This moment of plot is credible on a literal level as it shows what kind of actor Bob is (he later says he would prefer to be doing a play somewhere), but symbolically the show is dubbed from one language to another and the monkey is 'talking' and as such a portrayal of something not real; a different version; for the purposes of consumption. In the same scene Bob opens the door to a pseudo-prostitute who has been sent for his entertainment. Bob clearly is not interested. She proceeds to roll around on the floor, pretending to be a submissive slave in a fantasy role play. Not only does this scene work to provide humour and empathy for Bob, who wants and needs none of this, it once again underlines the central theme. The prostitute is *pretending* to do something. For Bob, he is being consumed and swamped in a world of surrealism which he desperately wants to escape.

Other moments of visual storytelling play out metaphors for the audience as the film's narrative accelerates. Bob is taking promotional shots for Suntory whisky, the photographer telling him to change his expression and pretend to be feeling something else. When he tastes the whisky he realises it is not real; probably coloured water. Bob is seen trying to exercise on skiing assimilation machine. Actress Kelly fumbles her way through an interview, talking utter rubbish, cut against visual scenes of Charlotte helping a group of traditionally dressed Japanese women to arrange flowers: a juxtaposition of the systematic, fake, and consumer-driven with beauty, tradition and nature. Charlotte continues her wandering and finds herself in a games arcade. Here she witnesses an onslaught of young, displaced characters interacting with the machines around them. They pretend to play the guitar, to shoot a gun, to fight, to dance in a club. This is a setting of hyper reality and mass simulation, inviting the audience to make sense of the thematic meaning behind the chosen images and relating them to the protagonists and their journeys.

Bob and Charlotte become close friends and decide to spend a night out together. Careful consideration of visual imagery continues as the audience is exposed to more symbolic and metaphorical allusions to the theme. In the first bar that Bob and Charlotte visit images of simulated fireworks are projected onto screens. Everyone sings karaoke and Charlotte decides to wear a pink wig, disguising her appearance and making her look like someone else.

Towards the end of the film when there is a fire alarm at the hotel, Bob and Charlotte stumble upon each other outside. This point of plot can be seen as not only a device used to push the two protagonists back together and share an intimate moment, but again it is symbolic of theme. It has been a false fire alarm, there is no fire, and so perhaps the audience is reminded the two are still caught up in a hyper-real world and need to be rescued.

On his day of departure from Tokyo, Bob receives another fax, this time a picture and the message 'I love you' from his daughter. This signals the end of Bob and Charlotte's time together; he has a family to go back to and be father for, but symbolically the image is yet another sign of the false world in which he lives. It is as if he is reminded that he has to go back to how things were, but does that mean he will return as the same man? Or will he return to his ordinary world having gained some new knowledge from his experience in Tokyo? Could Charlotte have provided elixir to help him survive?

Bob's entourage surround him as he leaves the hotel, asking if they can have a final picture of them all together. Bob agrees and so he stands there, an icon in the middle of a group of people who adopt fake smiles, helping to create in the photograph an image of what never was. But Bob has probably learned something, and no longer feels trapped in this world. On the way to the airport Bob asks the driver to stop as he sees Charlotte walking down a busy street. As they say their final good-byes probably the most memorable moment of film occurs, where Bob whispers into Charlotte's ears. She smiles, encouraged by his words, but the audience never hears what is said. This is a final epiphany to the film and the last moment of tremendous visual subtext: the audience does not need to hear what is said. It is left to their own imagination. Instead of allowing the secret to be told, the audience is denied access to this personal moment which cannot be transformed, transported, replicated, copied or destroyed.

5   Dialogue and Voice

Those not closely involved with screenwriting often believe the main task of forging a script is to write dialogue. In a screenplay, there is a lot of white on the page, with brief visual description and a fair amount of speech. However, much of what makes a script excel is 'invisible' work on structure, character and scene sculpting. Writing good dialogue is an important skill but by no means the only one. This chapter will look both at the role of dialogue within the screenplay, and how to achieve its effective expression.

Most amateur scripts are overwritten. There is too much dialogue, often with a lack of depth, conflict and pace. Screen dialogue is not real-life talk. It is sharper, more directed, highly constructed to fit story, layered with subtext and conflict, and though it may sound like a real conversation it is more like polished speech. It is common for screen-writers to note down as much as possible from their characters' mouths, before the words which sound so good are forgotten. This is no bad thing, and under these exciting, pressurised situations some of the best snatches of dialogue can emerge. What has to be remembered, however, is the process of re-writing which comes after this initial 'splurge', really stripping down the dialogue, making it function better and enhancing its texture. The more a writer develops an understanding of the characters and their psychology, the more the dialogue will develop. A character's need will change, and so too must the dialogue and its functions; a character's voice will emerge, resulting in shifting speech patterns; and a character's relationship with others will change, requiring a re-thinking of their exchanges. If a writer can understand what the functions of dialogue are, rather than purely approach the nuts and bolts of crafting it, then the writing process will become enriched and the screenplay will gain direction and substance.

The purpose of dialogue

Writers sometimes make the mistake of assuming that the primary role of dialogue is to provide information (content), whereas a more powerful approach is to view it as an exchange (relationship) where it is not just the words that carry meaning, but who speaks when, to whom and how. As demonstrated in Chapter 7 with the exercise *Saying Everything with Nothing*, the purpose of dialogue is not only to offer the audience information (commonly referred to as exposition) but to also reveal and define character, raise active dramatic and thematic questions, depict relationship dynamics, and establish tone, genre and world. Moving away from *dialogue-as-information* towards *dialogue-as-exchange*, these are useful questions to ask of a scene:

- Who is the character really talking to?
- What do they really want or need to say?
- What do they feel they cannot say, and why?
- Who is present in the scene that may be affecting what can or cannot be said?
- What is repressed (unsaid) rather than expressed?

A successful piece of dialogue which demonstrates the concept of dialogue-as-exchange is from US White House drama *The West Wing* (series three, episode three), a series which overflows and rejoices in its use of rhetoric. Bruno arrives to talk to Leo about helping with the new-election campaign and lays out his terms, some of which Leo refuses to agree to. Bruno warns him it is a 'deal-breaker'. Leo shrugs and tells him to talk to the President. As Bruno sits down in the Oval Office, President Bartlett uses almost identical words to the ones Bruno spoke to Leo a moment ago. But this time Bruno is on the receiving end and when he tries to protest, he is the one who is told it is a 'deal-breaker' and ends up having little choice but to agree. The scene illustrates that it is not so much the words but the emotional exchange they symbolise that is of importance. The words are identical in the two scenes, but it is how they are used, by whom and why, which changes their meaning, emphasising *context* over *content*. In good dialogue writing, two characters can seem to talk about the weather, a neighbour or their favourite colour, when what is really going underneath is that they are challenging each other, one trying to draw the other into a trap, or trying to tell each other how much they care and are sorry for what they did. A script which avoids dialogue which is 'on-the-nose' (stating the obvious) and instead allows space for the audience to figure the subtext out by themselves makes them active participants in the drama and therefore more likely to stay engaged.

Dialogue techniques

It is useful to consider good dialogue as that which is *repressed* rather than *expressed*, what is not said but implied. Dialogue is not just about words but also silences and the spaces in between, and sophisticated dialogue writing taking this into account offers a higher level of tension, conflict and character interaction; subtlety and suggestion create meaning over stating the obvious. There are a number of ways to approach dialogue as the *disruption* of conversation:

- Characters *lying* or not saying what they mean (consciously or subconsciously).
- Characters talking at *cross purposes* (not answering questions or listening).
- Characters *hinting* and insinuating rather than stating their case.
- Use of *silence* (to contrast or highlight emotion/situation/tension).
- Use of *key phrases* to highlight theme or character arc.

All these techniques can be used to highlight where the power lies in a scene, and how it shifts between characters as the scene progresses. As their very nature is about repressing information rather than expressing it, they automatically engage the audience further by making them want to know more. Good screenwriting is a constant balance between giving just enough information in order for the audience to stay attentive, without giving the game away so much they become bored. Using dialogue techniques which hold back rather than overstate are thus excellent ways of creating dramatic tension and rhythm, helping to improve scene writing and thematic resonance.

Two useful examples of silence in dialogue can be found in *Fargo* and *Kitchen Stories*. In *Fargo*, crooks Carl and Grimsrud form an odd couple, with Carl a jittery motormouth and Grimsrud a phlegmatic mute. Not only does this provide dark humour and an interesting character pairing, it also creates conflict as Carl increasingly feels Grimsrud is not pulling his weight. The partnership crumbles and at the end, Carl's fury about Grimsrud's unwillingness to communicate becomes his undoing, when he unleashes a volley of insults and Grimsrud responds, not with words, but action, killing him with an axe. Throughout the story, the audience thus finds out about Grimsrud mainly from his actions and behaviour, not his voice, and the relationship is portrayed through how they communicate, not what they say.

In *Kitchen Stories* social researcher Nilsson arrives to observe the daily life of irascible farmer Isak, and is expressly told not to enter into a social relationship with him but keep a professional distance. Most of the film is thus played out in silence or with very sparse dialogue, allowing rhythm, visual storytelling and small structural moments to tell the deeply poignant story of the men's developing friendship. It is a film worth studying in depth to analyse the potential uses of silence and how it can be surprisingly expressive.

The key phrase

A *key phrase* is a recurring and recognisable set of words used in different contexts during the course of a screenplay. It often has thematic meaning or resonance, and expresses characters' essential problems or issues. It can help to underscore character arc, relationships or plot mechanics depending on which character uses the phrase and in what context. An excellent screenwriting tool, it is an economical power bundle where the same words change and deepen their meaning. Each time a key phrase is used, it gathers impact and momentum and invites audience expectation that can be used by the writer as a kind of short hand. In this way, sometimes only a few words are necessary rather than a long speech, both audience and character coming to understand the importance, meaning and status of the key phrase. It can also be used ironically or for comic or suspense purposes, either fulfilling or twisting the expectations.

In *Strictly Ballroom*, there is a strong use of key phrases. There are three in the end sequence, all of which play a crucial part in the escalating climax. The primary thematic phrase that echoes throughout the script is 'live your life in fear' (which belongs mostly to Scott but is used both by Fran and Doug); 'bend your ear' (Doug's personal phrase and problem since no one pays him attention); and 'back in beginners where I belong' (Fran's essential problem). In the end sequence, Doug tries three times to 'bend [Scott's] ear', each time becoming more insistent and finally refusing to take no for an answer. When Fran confronts Scott with her disappointment at being ousted, she puts the boot in by using her key phrase ironically (echoed visually later as Scott watches Fran in a lacklustre dress in a mundane and uninspired beginners' dance, knowing he has failed not only himself but also her). The main phrase 'live your life in fear' is also expressed by Doug as a last plea to Scott as he struggles with his hardest choice at a key moment, and has tremendous resonance. It echoes inside Scott's head and is what finally makes him decide what to do. It is the phrase which haunts Scott throughout the second act and makes him change his mind in the climax and take the risk his mother never could, propelling the story towards the happy ending the audience yearns for.

Exposition

As David Howard articulates, in screenwriting the term *exposition* refers to:

> Information the audience needs in order to participate in and understand the events and relationships in the story. Exposition is information the characters already know but we don't...Where exposition departs from backstory is that it tends to be factual information rather than formative experience in the life of the character.
>
> (2004: 158)

The problem with exposition is two-fold: firstly, as information it can often feel dry and interrupt the flow of the narrative. A useful solution is to only provide it on a 'need-to-know' basis, when the writer has created enough dramatic interest to make the audience want to hear it. Secondly, the issue with information which characters know but the audience needs to find out is that it can feel stilted and unbelievable, as in real life we do not usually tell each other what we already know. Therefore, information needs to be offered in a way which feels credible to the characters' own situation; that they would have this exchange. A useful technique is to use questions or start a conversation halfway in, and use one character to 'force' the other character to offer up the information.

Exposition is particularly a problem in opening scenes, and *Toy Story* uses several techniques to overcome this. One is structural rhythm, where a large number of jokes interspersed through the information create laughs and breathers; another is by making characters argue over salient points, making it feel more natural and giving it dramatic drive. It is the device of the 'staff meeting', however, which allows for a natural expression of information. Even though the toys know about what is said here, the official staff meeting allows a comically pseudo-official imparting of information within credible relationships. It is structured so it contains not only important information (the move, Andy's birthday party) but also the irrelevant point of the Plastic Corrosion

Awareness meeting. This serves a number of functions as it is a lull between two longer, more important items; is funny and lets the audience relax and laugh; is a colourful detail that gives insight into the world of toys; makes the meeting seem to be for the toys not the audience; and creates three items, the strongest comic rhythm. The staff meeting naturally allows Woody (protagonist and current toy leader) to state important information both for plot and emotional purposes: reminding them to get Moving Buddies serves to highlight that toys can get lost (which later happens to Buzz and Woody); the birthday party reveals their main fear is to be replaced or discarded ('toy death'); and Woody calms their anxiety by reminding them that what really matters is to be there for their child. In a short space of time the audience has been told, in a comic manner relevant to the genre, the characters' main fear and problem, their deeper purpose, and that Woody is a good leader. Exposition is deftly handled so it feels natural, engaging and important; providing emotional story information as well as plot fact.

Writing dialogue

Bad dialogue can obliterate a script. If the story is well structured and the character's emotional journey well developed, it can still be let down by flat, wooden, clunky dialogue. The art of dialogue writing lies in the ability to give it function and texture, but make it unaware of itself and natural for the audience; it should run like water. As Aronson points out, 'dialogue is not like real life conversation at all. It is a very tightly and carefully structured illusion of conversation' (2001: 256). The key word here is *illusion*; it must seem normal, but have other powers (function, texture, personality, polish). As it is also important that the style of dialogue should fit with the world and tone of the story, 'good dialogue' is not necessarily set in stone. However, the following provides some useful guidelines.

In most cases, every word of dialogue in a screenplay should count. Screen time is precious so there is no room for wasted exchanges or superfluous waffle. The words spoken by characters are directed at advancing the story. In scenes, they function to progress the beat of action; they are a way of making the scene turn. The dialogue feeds from and into the story, pulling characters along their physical and emotional journeys. Dialogue reveals intention and decision-making by characters, supporting their step-by-step growth within the narrative as a whole. Once the context of a scene is established, the dialogue enables it to be explored, expressing feeling, attitude and story value to shape the direction to the scene's heart. The flow of dialogue in a scene should be considered carefully. Some of how dialogue is structured will be reliant upon subtext and hidden agenda (see below), but in general it is worth spending time thinking about how dialogue can be layered. If a scene is built in a rigid, monotonous way, literally a structure of question/answer/question/answer, the audience will switch off. Rather, patterns of speech can be structured to tease out the story in interesting ways and use knowledge of character and voice to create texture.

Subtext

When we speak in real life, we often know what we are saying. We have an idea of the direction our conversation is going in, and what we want out of it. We bring an agenda to the conversation, which may be to make a point, make someone say something, or create a feeling or atmosphere among the people taking part. Sometimes, however, we dare not say what we want, so say something else instead. This is *subtext*; the meaning beneath the words. Characters in a screenplay are no different. In fact, if a character has to drive the story through a series of scenes, trying to get what they want, then it could be argued that fictional characters are even more reliant on subtext. It can be very revealing, paving the way to a deeper understanding of the story and the character's place within it. Two characters may be having a rather innocuous conversation about the television, but what they are really saying is much more: the characters will use the opportunity of talking about the set, the colour, brightness, channels available, shows currently playing – whatever – as a way of hinting at something else. It may be a couple, seemingly talking about how the volume is too loud but actually talking about how their relationship is not going to work. It may be a brother and a sister, arguing about which channel to watch, but subtextually revealing that one is always favoured by their parents. For the audience it can be more rewarding and often more intriguing to hear the story told via subtext. Blatant, on-the-nose dialogue can serve its purpose on some occasions, but the audience gets more involved in hearing conversations which mask other conversations. *Concealment* is a key component of subtext; the surface words cover the intended, subtextual ones. Subtext can often be linked to *fear*, where characters are afraid of revealing true feelings or saying what they think at this stage in the story. Consider this exchange, taking place after a first date:

```
EXT. STREET - NIGHT
MARK and CARL walk down the street. Slight tension
between the two.
They reach MARK's car. MARK looks at KARL.
They both smile. Slight awkwardness.
                    MARK
          Well this is me.
                    KARL
                    (re: the car)
          Nice.
Silence, awkwardness.
                    KARL
          Had it long?
                    MARK
          A year. Just less.
                    KARL
          I've always liked that model.
                    MARK
          It's different isn't it?
                    KARL
          Good on fuel I hear.
```

Both the characters want to know how the other feels about the date, but instead of broaching the topic, they talk about the car. Although Mark and Karl are discussing the car's credentials, what they are really doing is delaying the ultimate question 'will I see you again?' and hinting their feelings to one another via the medium of the car. Subtextually, the two characters *fear* the other saying no and so partake in a diverted conversation to delay and fish for the outcome.

Subtext is also imbued with *power*. Characters bring agendas to the conversation which are pushed via the means of subtext, directing not only the conversation but the reactions of other participants so that what is being pushed is accepted. In this way we can understand subtext as a *rhetorical device,* a means of persuading those involved to follow the line of thought (agenda) but by concealing it to make it appear as normal speech. Subtext can therefore be very powerful; it can give a character a great deal of ammunition with which to load a conversation. Sometimes this is common in a villain, who uses his 'gift of the gab' to persuade others of the hero's inadequacies. This is his way of trying to stop the hero achieving his goal, turning people against him by cleverly using speech to create a negative impression. Of course in this instance the ability would lie in him dealing the subtext in such a way that his listeners would have no idea of his real intentions; he must be a master of speech. Subsequently, apart from the context of subtext itself, delivery is also important. This includes *speech patterns*, *rhythm*, *vocabulary*, *silences*, *looks* and *gestures*. All these elements of delivery hold the power to successfully apportion the intended agenda. Subtext does not always have negative intentions – it can work quite the opposite – but in whatever context, the outcome is always rhetorical.

The case for subtext is that it is relative to character and personality, and it fuels the beat of story that a scene functions to explore. Character intentions and motivations are evident from subtext, giving the audience a discreet way of understanding how characters feel and what they are trying to achieve. Subtext is also crucial in that it creates layers of conflict; implicit agendas which battle to reach the fore, enriching the flow and feel of the narrative. What is unsaid is left to the audience's active interpretation.

Subtext is used with both ironic and comedic effect in Woody Allen's *Annie Hall*, where characters' subtextual thoughts are provided as captions to the audience, demonstrating how when someone says one thing, what they actually think is another. In the following extract, Alvy and Annie talk nervously on her rooftop terrace; they like each other but fear saying so. Though an extreme and unusual example, it highlights perfectly the juxtaposition between spoken word and underlying meaning (captions are underscored).

```
              ALVY
              (pointing toward the
              apartment after a short
              pause)
          So, did you do shoot the
          photographs in there or what?

              ANNIE
              (Nodding, her hand on her
              hip)
          Yeah, yeah, I sorta dabble around,
          you know.
```

Annie's thoughts pop on the screen as she talks: **I dabble?
Listen to me - what a jerk!**

> ALVY
> They're...they're...they're
> wonderful, you know. They have
> ... they have, uh...a...a
> quality.

As do Alvy's: **You are a great-looking girl**

> ANNIE
> Well, I-I-I would-I would like
> to take a serious photography
> course soon.

Again, Annie's thoughts pop on: **He probably thinks I'm
a yo-yo**

> ALVY
> Photography's interesting, 'cause,
> you know, it's-it's a new art form,
> and a, uh, a set of aesthetic
> criteria have not emerged yet.

And Alvy's: **I wonder what she looks like naked?**

> ANNIE
> Aesthetic criteria? You mean,
> whether it's, uh, good photo or
> not?

I'm not smart enough for him. Hang in there

> ALVY
> The-the medium enters in as a
> condition of the art form itself.
> That's-

I don't know what I'm saying - she senses I'm shallow

> ANNIE
> Well, well, I...to me-I...I
> mean, it's-it's-it's all
> instinctive, you know. I mean,
> I just try to uh, feel it, you
> know? I try to get a sense of
> it and not think about it so much.

God, I hope he doesn't turn out to be a shmuck like the others

<pre>
                        ALVY
            Still, still we- You need a set of
            aesthetic guide lines to put it in
            social perspective, I think.
</pre>

Christ, I sound like FM radio. Relax

They're quiet for a moment, holding wine glasses and sipping.

Writing and voice

Screenwriters write for a voice; screenwriters write with a voice. Although the former idea is easily understood, the latter may be somewhat complex. Writing with a voice considers the screenwriter's own voice, and how to portray this sense of authorship via a body of work (types of ideas) and tone (writing technique). This is discussed further in Chapter 12, but for now we would like to approach voice from two angles: writing for a character and writing for a world.

Writing for a voice

The dialogue that characters speak reflects their personality; thus, voice plays a crucial part. Dialogue and voice are character-driven, the way they express themselves in given situations being a quick and effective way of representing character and personality. Characters' voices are unique and individual and stem from backstory, attitude, point of view, circumstance, sociology. In this way character voice is a verbal metaphor for the internal state, just as the visual image can be symbolic of story theme. Not only this, character voice is an effective way of making a screenplay distinct. It has the power to grab an audience by the ears and make claims for originality. Thus, writing for a voice – the character's verbal expression of personality – is an art in itself.

When constructing a character voice, there are three different aspects to consider. First is *vocabulary* – what kind of words they use, if they use slang and how issues of class, race, gender and sexuality may present themselves. Second is *rhythm* – what kind of sentence construction do the characters use? Do they speak a lot or a little? Do they always finish their sentences or leave them hanging? Do they use a lot of questions; are they long-winded; clear and concise or mumbling and rambling? The personal syntax of characters can speak volumes about who they are, not just the words they choose but the patterns they present them in. Third is *attitude* – how do the characters use their dialogue: as a weapon? As a way of flattering, agreeing and smoothing over conflict? As a way of gleaning information? Barking orders? Are they confident or shy, positive or negative? What is the purpose of talking for these characters and what do they reveal of themselves, overall or in a particular situation, through the *manner* in which they speak?

In an attempt to purport a strong sense of character voice, writers can use techniques such as playing around with syntax, referencing popular culture, alluding to common expressions and even inventing new words or phrases. This can result in engaging pieces of dialogue, which although have to stay true to character, can add life and dynamism. Voice-led dialogue, whereby the character's personality dictates how they speak, can add peaks and troughs to the sound of a scene, giving it vocal pace and texture. If the construction of individual scenes and sequences builds the pace of a screenplay, then the construction of dialogue and expression can build the pace of a scene (or single exchange).

American television drama *Sex and the City* is a useful example for discussing notions of character voice because it cleverly plays around with expression. This is partly due to the show having Carrie Bradshaw (a writer) as narrator, empowering the audience with words of wisdom and creating emotional impact. It also has a rich ensemble of characters who possess highly different personalities and verbalise their individual identities.

In *Anchors Away* (series five, episode one), the girls are eating brunch and talking about lovers. When it is hinted to Miranda (sarcastic workaholic with a dim view on romance) that Steve has been her only true love, she snipes that he was hardly a 'core shaker'. Here the character uses the word 'core' to mean heart and 'shaker' to mean throb, the phrase sounding more interesting and original than 'heart throb' that everyone knows. It fits the character too, giving a sarcastic tone to something potentially positive. Later, when Carrie gives her obligatory episode summing up, the phrase is rearticulated. She says that Miranda's non-core shaker came to the rescue when she was 'shaken to the core'. Like the show's narrative, the expression (key phrase) comes full circle, though in an altered way, and gives bite to the sharp and sassy dialogue which is a common feature of this drama. In another scene Carrie states she is going shopping. Rather than saying she is 'going to spend money' she says she is going to 'throw some much needed money downtown'. In this instance the expression is simply a playing around of syntax, offering the audience a new way of saying 'spending money'. It also fits the character, a spendaholic, with tones of sarcasm and self-awareness about how for some she is simply throwing her money away.

An interesting word invention is later used when Samantha (brash, sex-driven, overtly dominant) complains about 'lover' Richard, who has cheated on her. She says the man is 'dangerous and toxic', to which Carrie astutely replies 'so he's Manthrax?' This is a clear reference to Anthrax, which the audience has knowledge of as a toxic and dangerous substance, personifying it to Richard. Again, this line leaps from the text, a sign of original, quirky and clever dialogue. As Charlotte (mild, meek, old-fashioned romantic) walks down the street with gay friend Anthony, she reveals it has been six months since she had sex. Anthony is distraught and warns her about passing the six months mark; after that it is a 'sleigh ride into menopause'. As well as creating obvious camp humour befitting Anthony's demeanour, this remark is highly original and creates a strong visual image. The fact that the menopause is linked to Christmas is also unexpected and humorous.

The episode is littered with references to commonly used social phrases, creating a sense of textured, lively dialogue which generates relevant audience appeal. Sheltering from the sudden pouring of rain, Carrie spots a nice looking guy. Upset at being drenched, she remarks 'it can go from bad, to cute'. Later, when the four women are at a sailors' party, Samantha flirts cheekily: 'Ahoy, matey'. This theme is continued when Carrie, feeling dejected, moans that 'this ship has sailed and tragically I'm still on it'. The use here of common expressions which are appropriated to both the sea theme and the characters' circumstances add an overall sense of dynamism, and work to make the audience see the connections and celebrate them.

These examples demonstrate how screenwriters can use the power of character voice to create interesting, dynamic and enriched drama. Character expression can certainly define a personality, at the same time ensuring that the overall experience of dialogue is fulfilling and memorable. This can be seen as a common trend which, we propose, will develop even more so. If we think visually for a moment, strides have been made in film and television to develop and enhance what an audience *sees*. Visual techniques such as split screens, flashbacks, flo-mo, freeze-frame and CGI (Computer Generated Imagery) have been instilled to challenge, satisfy and 'hold the attention of an audience whose powers of concentration [have been] diminished' (Nelson, 1997: 30). With this in mind, it could be suggested that screen dialogue should follow the same pattern to enhance what an audience *hears*. In a world saturated with written and verbal communication, from magazines and music to mobile phones, text messaging and Internet chat rooms, words have lost their meaning; phrases have become redundant. It is perhaps inevitable that audiences want to be challenged in what they hear, just like they crave seeing the next visual spectacle. The screenwriter's role is to understand and integrate this. If visual screen techniques have been developed and enhanced to *stimulate the eye*, then dialogue is being developed and enhanced to *stimulate the ear*.

Voicing the world

It is not only individual characters that require a specific voice but often the world as a whole. Each world has its own way of communicating, a 'voice of the story', which is the task of the writer to unearth and bring to light. As seen above, the *Sex and the City* characters inhabit a particular world and though they have their own individual voices, they share a similar tone and style – modern, urban, sassy, female. The way characters speak as an ensemble can add depth, credibility and sophistication to the narrative experience, and give further information about who belongs in the world or its various subsets. In *Mean Girls*, the high school as a whole has a particular way of speaking but even more so the various cliques within it, all with their own syntax and vocabulary. When newcomer Cady arrives in the school it is a whole new world, an unknown jungle which she has to learn the rules of in order to socially survive. Dialogue and language become a key currency, as Regina, leader of A-list girls 'The Plastics' tells her sycophantic followers what they can and cannot say, just as she tells them what they can or cannot wear. As Cady develops through the story, not only does she adopt their look but also their way of speaking and their value system, illustrating her inner change.

In *Fargo*, the small town world is at odds with the thriller-style plot of kidnap and murder, creating both comedy and pathos. Most of the characters, including protagonists Jerry and Marge, belong to the world of ordinary folk living everyday lives. The hired kidnappers clearly do not, however, and speak very differently, using different accents, vocabulary and sentence construction. They come from another place, signifying their outsider status in terms of moral values, expected behaviour and rogue dramatic element; they are the fly in the ointment, that which does not fit, and by entering into their world and inviting them to enter his, Jerry makes his cosy world crumble.

The construction of a voice for the world can be subtle and inconspicuous, but in some cases it is consciously innovative, as in HBO television series *Deadwood*. Here a distinct voice for the whole series and its frontier-town Western world was devised through a surprisingly effective and original collision of Shakespearian tongue in raw and violent mouths. This offers a fresh and unusual perspective on a familiar genre, creating associations of tragedy and theatricality, big minds battling for power in a small space, expanding the thematic territory way beyond the generic expectations of a conventional Western.

6 The Cultures of Screenwriting

Industry culture

There are three distinctly different areas a screenwriter may currently choose to work in, and it is important to understand the conventions and expectations in each in order to make informed decisions about working practices and career choices. This chapter looks at traditional areas of importance: cinema, television and short film; but in the fast changing climate of the media world, new conventions and arenas are also emerging, as discussed in Chapter 13. Genre is also discussed in this chapter, both in industry and writerly contexts. For further essential insight into industry practices, we recommend *The Screenwriter's Survival Guide* (US based) and *The UK Film Finance Handbook* (UK based), and regular reading of publications such as *Screen International* (feature film), *Broadcast* (UK television) and *ScriptWriter Magazine.*

Cinema

The main aim of many screenwriters is to write feature scripts. It is a viable goal but a hugely competitive one. Feature films cost vast sums of money to make and many people – producers, directors, actors, script editors, development executives – demand input and changes to scripts. This is discussed at length both below (working with others) and in Chapter 13 (understanding the costing of ideas within the feature industry). It is crucial that serious screenwriters learn as much as they can about the industry; even relatively low budget features come with a large industry machine attached, and the writer must be professional in approach and understand the intended market. Film is the creative writing form most closely allied to business, and writers cannot afford to be too precious about what they may consider 'their art' but instead find ways to work with conventions in ways that best fit them. However, Chapter 13 looks at possibilities of working against convention and still forging a successful career (by 'successful' we mean a script is produced, not whether it results in commercial success).

Different countries have different cultures of feature film production, how the industry is shaped, and attitudes to writers and film ideas. In the USA, most films are either independently produced or financed by studios, whereas in the UK, government funding is still common. France is a good example of how distribution strategies have attempted to protect national cinema output in mainstream cinemas. Whatever the country, many types of production company exist, with their own agenda and style, and it is important that writers find the right producer for a script. Writers should dedicate time to research the market and find producers whose tastes converge with their story, and focus pitching and promotion to these producers in the first instance.

One general and unfortunate culture within the film industry is the low status of the screenwriter. Though films rarely exist without a script, cinema is largely seen as a director's medium, and the screenwriter is usually not awarded authorship status or even allowed on set or into the editing room. Take a moment to consider this – how many screenwriters' names roll off the tongue as easily as directors'? Even screenwriters themselves can be more familiar with directors than writers, and many producers treat screenwriters as a replaceable commodity. It is commonplace within the feature film industry to buy an idea off one writer and hire another to script it; to sack a writer from a project and replace them with a new writer, or two, or five; or bring in writers who specialise in action sequences, comedy or dialogue. To understand the full impact of such industry conventions on the writer and their practice, compare this with other forms of writing: imagine a novel written by five different authors, each of whom had little contact with the previous one; or a poem receiving a final polish by a specialist in rhythm or metaphor. These examples sound faintly ludicrous yet highlight how differently both public and industry view authorship in fiction, poetry and playwriting as opposed to screenwriting. Even television, which in the UK has long-standing connections to radio and theatre, has a higher opinion of writers than cinema, and has traditionally offered them greater authorial status and opportunity.

Television

Television writing differs in substantial ways from the big screen. If screenwriters are lucky enough to land a TV commission at the beginning of their careers, this will nearly always be on a series created by another writer. Therefore writers have to be able to write dialogue and storylines for characters they may not know well, and do so to very tight deadlines. Television writing is faster and more high pressured than feature film writing, but also offers the opportunity to have work produced more quickly; a feature can take years to reach the screen, and may never be released even if it has been produced. Regular TV series tend to have a distinct house style or 'series recipe' which writers have to adhere to, while offering their own ideas and creativity. Working to brief is a major feature of television writing, and can be a great discipline. Some writers view television writing as 'lower ranking' than feature film but this is often no longer the case, as proven in the USA by numerous highly successful HBO series such as *Six Feet Under* and *The Sopranos*. The culture of television writing is changing and offers more scope to the modern writer, though it has also been dented by the trend for documentary drama and reality TV (see Chapter 9). Creating ideas for new TV *series* or *serials* (the former is self-contained episodes in a recurring situation, the latter a continuing story told over a finite number of episodes) is a different discipline to feature ideas. Though there are similarities, with story built from world, theme and genre, instead of focusing on building structure, TV series demand attention to character. Character is what gives a TV series 'legs'; the ability to become long-running, and therefore economically successful.

Creating interesting character pairings and relationship dynamics is the lifeblood of TV series, and should be approached as a distinct form. If new writers want to attempt creating a TV series, they must be aware of conventions in production as well as how to pitch and present a project through a 'Bible'. As turnaround is relatively fast, producers have to know they can rely on writers to deliver and so it is highly unlikely that original series are commissioned by unproven writers. The more common path is freelance work writing episodes on existing series, promoted to hired staff to create storylines and characters in development conferences, and after further years of experience, the opportunity to pitch original series. TV writers have to take a long-term view and work on projects they may not feel artistically close to in order to develop relationships, experience and technique. As Pamela Douglas attests, 'television series aren't bought and sold on ideas, but the ability to deliver on those ideas' (2007: 34).

Short film

It could be argued that short film is not really an industry as it rarely makes any money. However, in the career of a screenwriter, the short film can be a crucial and productive step and needs to be examined to see what it can offer. Many screenwriters cut their teeth on short scripts as it allows manageable bite-size narratives where writers can practice craft and explore voice. There are two different approaches to the short form: seeing it as a 'miniature-feature' with classical three act narrative, or approaching the form in its own right with an opportunity to explore other types of narratives and structures. This second approach is discussed further in Chapter 9. Whichever is chosen, the short script offers screenwriters an opportunity to practice creation and honing of craft, a possibility to have work produced and gain a greater understanding of the script-to-screen relationship, and career building through training and development schemes, festivals and competitions.

As screenwriting is only ever the blueprint to a film, it is imperative that screenwriters gain experience of the production process to judge for themselves what works on screen. Occasionally a script can read beautifully on the page, yet still not gel as a film, and the more a writer can experience their work in its final form, the more they will learn about what works well. Without ever seeing a script transformed into film, a writer is unlikely to become as adept as is necessary. The other benefit in having a short script made is that writers learn about the realities and restrictions of production. However much money a project attracts, there is never enough and cuts always have to be made. Part of becoming a professional screenwriter is giving the producer and director rewrites demanded by practicalities; a new location has to be found, a character dropped, an act break revised. Screenwriters need to be creative and hardworking, not only during initial development with their own ideas but also during pre-production when reality forces their hand and demands skill under pressure. This is common in feature film production as well as television, and gaining experience of it on a smaller scale with shorts is invaluable.

The short script also allows screenwriters to build a career by becoming known to industry. Though there is little money in short film, it offers value in other ways. In the UK and Europe, government arts agencies and film funding bodies regularly look for upcoming writers, as do development executives and production houses. Everyone wants to discover hot-young talent or a fresh new voice, which means that film and television industries have many networking practices in place to support and nurture talent. As short films are relatively cheap to make, especially with digital production (see Chapter 13), funders are more willing to take a risk. New writers have the chance to build relationships and create a name for themselves through sending work to writing competitions, short film production schemes, and submitting independently produced work to festivals. The short film can thus function as an excellent stepping stone to breaking into the industry as well as quickly improving craft.

Working with industry

An often unspoken aspect of screenwriting is how to work productively with people during development. Unlike many other forms of creative writing, scripts are developed through some form of collaboration, even if written by one writer. It is unusual for a screenwriter not to work closely with a script editor, and producers will often have a great deal of input into the shaping of drafts. Many writers mistakenly assume they can write their script and sell it, whereas the reality of the industry is that development is a long process of honing a script with the help (or sometimes hindrance) of others. Even directors and cast sometimes wish to have a say, and writers must be able to handle input and work with it to reshape the script into an improved rather than dissipated draft. One of the main problems a writer can face is to be given a multitude of notes by different development personnel who do not always communicate with each other. Notes may conflict or compete with each other in terms of priority. An occasional problem is that producers are not adept enough at analysing scripts, and provide false or unhelpful solutions. It is thus the job of the writer to pick their way through the morass of comments and find the truth behind them. Rather than follow notes blindly, it is important to discern what they are really saying – the 'subtext' of the feedback – then address it in the most effective and relevant way. This can be difficult and something that comes with experience, though an effective way to learn for novice writers can be by working in writers' groups (see Chapter 13). As rewrites are a big element of screenwriting (first drafts are often seen as contributing about 20% to the final script), writers must learn how to work effectively with notes and the working practices and demands of producers. Screenwriters have to accept that rewriting is not a symptom of something done badly, but a natural part of the process. A key aspect to the culture of development, therefore, is working creatively with feedback, and as this skill is often not addressed in training, an in-depth discussion is offered in Chapter 8.

The script reader

As production companies and funding agencies are sent huge volumes of scripts (and plays, novels and treatments), they hire extra personnel

6

82

Foundations

as the first port of call for this work. The script reader is often hired as a freelance assistant and can work for one or numerous companies. It is useful for writers to understand the role of the reader as they can have great impact on a script's progress. Though a reader is a relatively lowly figure on the development ladder with no power to approve a project, they are able to say no, and can turn away a script before it reaches the executives who award funding. Script readers read all types of material and write script reports (known as *coverage* in the USA). The exact form this takes varies from company to company, but mainly it comprises a log line, a brief half page or page synopsis, and two to three pages of comments on idea, story, structure, characters, writing craft, tone and potential. The reader submits the report to the development executive and sometimes attends development meetings where it is decided which writers will be invited to a meeting or to send another draft. Occasionally projects that are rough around the edges make it through if they have an interesting, fresh and exciting idea, or if talent of interest is attached (writer, director, producer or cast).

For budding writers, working as a script reader is an excellent way to learn about the industry, hone writing skills and network with influential development personnel. In the beginning of a career, many writers feel their scripts are unique, and expect special treatment. After working as a reader, it becomes clear why it often takes two or three months for a writer to get a reply to their submission and why it is so important to make sure the work is in good shape before sending it out. Working in a development office almost becomes a visual metaphor for writers, its tall stacks of manuscripts teetering on the edge of every available surface. It is a timely reminder that there are thousands of writers all clamouring for a limited pot of money, and learning from the inside about commissioning, development and decision making can serve as fast-track training in the reality of professional screenwriting, giving greater chances of success. Script reading also provides on-the-job guidance in how not to write; by reading hundreds of scripts, writers come to see common mistakes and over-familiar story patterns, gaining an intuitive sense of what makes a story work.

The culture of genre

Genre is a key culture of screenwriting. More than ever, film (and increasingly, television) is produced and packaged according to a set of genres which the audience understands, attaches itself to and subsequently demands. Robert McKee notes that 'the audience is already a genre expert. It enters each film armed with a complex set of anticipations learned through a lifetime of moviegoing' (1999: 80). This suggests that genre is mainly employed because of audience; it is their satisfaction that is required. Glen Creeber argues that genre is 'the product of a text- and audience-based negotiation activated by the viewer's expectation' (2001: 7), again pointing to the relationship between genre and audience. Genre is essential in marketing, ensuring that dramas are packaged according to audience demand and sold to specific demographics. This is evident in the way that films, especially, are trailered; audience types are targeted, with the story and style offered in quick, easily digestible segments announcing what kind of film it is. However, although mar- ketability can be seen to dictate screenwriting culture, for the writer the concerns are somewhat different. Attaining a suitable genre in writing comes not only from employing the correctly coloured ele- ments of a screenplay (story type, characters, visual grammar) but by presenting an appropriate overall audience experience. Torben Grodal offers interesting insights here, purporting that the cognitive and per- ceptual processes of watching a screen drama (understanding the story, grasping character motivations) are intimately linked with emotional processes (1997: 1). This practice is seen as psychosomatic, affecting both mind and body, and is intrinsically linked to genre because of the range of feelings it can generate. For Grodal, 'some feelings may be generated from interior sources, but in visual fiction even feelings with interior sources, like memory, have to be cued by some exterior means' (Ibid.: 2). In other words, the narrative structure and narrative flow of a particular genre possesses the ability to produce a certain emotional response in its audience. What this means for the screenwriter is that although the codes and conventions of a genre are important in the drama's make-up, they are nothing if the audience does not respond emotionally in a pattern that befits the genre. For example, a thriller film will aim to put fear into the audience and invite them to live the narrative subjectively, in which they too feel threatened along with the vulnerable, passive protagonist. Screwball comedies on the other hand take a more objective stance, the audience watching from a distance and responding to the characters with pity, embarrassment and a feel- ing of safety away from the funny yet awful situation. These emotional responses are brought about by the combination of generic codes and conventions (Grodal's 'exterior means') used by the screenwriter; they come together to *create* the emotion, not just sit alongside it. For these reasons, genre places huge demands on the act of screenwriting.

Genre and structure

Genre has an important influence on the type of story a screenplay will offer, and dictates how the story is told. As discussed, screenplays are journeys undertaken by characters, and the emotional development they encounter from physical action. This basic concept underpins all narratives, and employing a particular genre will hold this at heart but shape it in a distinctive way and give it a specific direction. This is where genre becomes a *tool* for the screenwriter. It is not necessarily a paradigm into which genre films have to be pushed, but a way of helping to develop writing into a shape which works for the genre in question. Understanding how genre functions as a concept and how specific elements of the narrative change accordingly is a productive approach for a screenwriter; not viewing it as rigid constraints onto what can and cannot be done. Elemental devices to be worked with in story structure include *dramatic shape, dramatic goal, inciting incident, conflict* and *climax*. As an example, in the romantic comedy the dramatic shape is almost always about the chase between two lovers. They work like protagonist and antagonist to one other, wanting yet rejecting each other. The dramatic goal is to be united with the other; often it starts as a chase from one side, which eventually develops into mutual love. The inciting incident is relative to this goal in that the two lovers meet and 'unmeet,' and from this moment on, the chase begins. If they did not meet there would be no chase; similarly, if there was no rejection or 'unmeeting' there would be no need for a chase. The main bulk of the narrative is driven by the conflict of the two lovers colliding and reacting to each other. For the majority of the story they are in conflict (though this may be one sided), pushing each other's patience and pulling each other in uncomfortable directions. Because of the comedic element to this genre, the conflict provides humour; the audience laughs at the star-crossed lovers and cringes at the situations they find themselves in. The climax of the romantic comedy comes in the form of a well-awaited reunion of the lovers. The audience has seen the story develop from bad to worse to unbelievable, when a final event brings the two back together (possibly a mirror scene of the inciting incident) and they realise they are in love and right for each other.

The sports film demonstrates a dramatic shape usually in the form of a rites of passage, where a protagonist faces a problem and grows out of it into a new person who proves their value to the world. The dramatic goal of sports films is in the winning of a game or sporting event, by which we understand the playing of sport as an extension of inner anguish needing to be exorcised. Winning the game is symbolic of coming to terms with the inner self, and making that passage into a new, improved person. The inciting incident can come when the protagonist joins the team, sometimes reluctantly, or when the main sporting challenge is set. Conflict throughout embodies both inner and outer turmoil. Emotionally, the protagonist battles with who they are and what they are worth, this often taking place in the home environment. Sometimes they clash with teammates, as a symbolic link to the physical conflict. The protagonist (sometimes whole team) makes mistakes and loses matches, endangering the prospects of winning the eventual prize. This prize is the climax of the film, where a substantial, special match takes place. The setting needs to be larger and more critical than usual, with more at stake for the protagonist (team) to prove. The climax may come in the form of winning the match or event, but can also come by losing; either way, the protagonist overcomes their inner turmoil and thus triumphs. The sport is thrown aside and the emotional rewards reaped.

As these case studies demonstrate, genre as a set of defined rules does not have to impose negatively on the screenwriting process. Rather, it can be seen to guide the creative interpretation of elements. Dramatic shape, goal, inciting incident, conflict and climax are moments in which genre demands specific attention, but that is not to say they have to be formulaic or clichéd. Instead they become helpful signposts to work with in ways that best suit the project, to ensure it finds the relevant path through the story.

Genre and character

Genre can place similar requisites on the types of character experienced with a narrative, namely, *protagonist* and *antagonist*. Like story and structure, the basic element of these will remain the same: the protagonist is the hero whose point of view the audience adopts, and whose physical and emotional journey they align with; the antagonist is the villain or main challenge to the hero, who appears to stop the journey and try to defeat their hope of achieving the goal. What genre does for character is recommend that these character functions are played by archetypes the audience can recognise and connect with. In Westerns, the protagonist usually takes the form of lone hero or wandering nomad, often a cowboy or gunfighter. This archetype travels from town to town, often with a chip on their shoulder, venting anger on the bad and evil. The function they serve is to triumph good over evil (or their perception of it) and rather than take residence in the town with the grateful people, they move on. The antagonist of the Western is often somebody who has let personal greed or power overrule their moral conduct. Even in more modern Westerns with so-called anti-heroes, where the antagonist can be somebody of high social and seemingly respectable standing, the battle is often over moral ground, and the protagonist embodies the values that belong to the land (at times wilderness), whereas the antagonist carries the potential corruptive influences of civilisation.

Science fiction films operate in a similar way, often employing a lone hero protagonist who wants to save the world. In this genre, their battle is with aliens or other non-human forms which represent the fear (or hope) for the future of mankind. The protagonist often has internal wounds which drive the emotion and use the physical battles and confrontations with alien forms and technology as a way of expressing this inner angst. As the plot develops, so does the understanding of themselves and their dramatic problem. Like the Western, protagonists in science fiction are usually faced with a climactic showdown with the major antagonist towards the end of the film. This represents a final battle with the inner self and a cleansing of internal wounds. Indeed, it could be argued that the science fiction film is a modern day reworking of the Western, with its concerns of exploring frontiers, attempting civilisation or colonisation, taming the wild, and coming into contact with the 'other.' Therefore their core protagonist arcs and dramatic questions are often startlingly similar.

Genre and visual imagery

When the concept of genre is introduced in teaching situations, most students think of visual signifiers, considering the look of a film and mise-en-scène as elements which point to a particular type. Visual imagery which alludes to genre is certainly important, but in many ways comes second to story, structure and character. This actually aligns to the more general screenwriting process: the first and foremost part of screenplay development relates to creating story and structure, and developing characters to tell this story effectively. It could thus be suggested that the true nature of genre – what really *makes* it a particular type – lies with story and plot. It is only in the next phase, when the screenplay is written, that visual imagery comes into play.

Metaphorically speaking, story and plot are the genetic code of genre while visual imagery (and to some extent dialogue) is physical appearance; the dressing up.

Visual imagery, or visual grammar, refers to the ways genre is physically positioned on screen. The imagery acts as an instant signifier of genre just like signs and symbols are used in culture to represent ideas and rules. Dark tones, a boiling kettle and a spilt drawer of knives in *Dolores Claiborne* are indicative of the thriller in the same way that a brightly decorated, ultra-modern minimalist office in the middle of Soho speaks trendy and creative. They are both semiotic displays of environment, tone and attitude, invoking the user to interact accordingly. In film and television, visual motifs are used to denote how the audience should understand the frame and respond emotionally. These elements which a screenwriter, and subsequently design team and director, work with include *colour*, *object* and *costume*. Colour is a general term which embodies how genre can be depicted by the look and feel that is presented. It does not stand alone, but is an umbrella for elements such as set design, costume and lighting. Together they form a visual palette evocative of the genre in question. For example, a psychological thriller will be presented as dark and eerie. This can be brought about by dark clothing, dark settings and shadowy lighting which masks people's full faces. In turn, this creates a mood of unease and discomfort, where nothing is plainly obvious or as it seems. In contrast, a fantasy adventure story might adopt a brighter, more colourful tone to represent the optimistic, utopian sense of the world, brought about by awesome landscapes, regal costumes and dazzling lighting effects. For children especially, this would induce an escapist fantasy in which they could live their dreams.

Objects are also a useful way of alluding to genre, both as part of the environment and the way characters interact with them. If in a thriller a victim is under threat from the crazed killer, it would be credible they grab a knife for protection. This object is symbolic of danger and death, and works in a thriller because it instills in the audience a clear sense of danger and threat. Not only does it carry visual weight to reinforce the codes expected, it speaks its own language by inferring the situation that the character is in; desperate. This could also be argued of the mask that conceals the killer's identity, as seen in the *Scream* trilogy. Credible to the narrative, it follows the genre's genealogy as a likely item, but also says much about the situation the characters are faced with. It tells the audience that behind the mask may be someone who the victim actually knows, and the fear comes not only from the impending death, but death from the unknown. This is likely to involve the audience assimilating the scenario and anticipating their own fear, which works to create the emotional response that genre requires.

The visual discourse offered by costume is also effective in depicting genre. Clothes worn and accessories carried act as a stage upon which generic traits are performed, the audience using visual semiotics as a quick and effective way of accessing the signified. Costumes can be evocative of period, class, status, mood and situation, and in this way are seen as storyteller. The sports kit worn in a sports film not only depicts the obvious joining of a team, but the commitment the character has made to the narrative by entering a new world and experiencing a new set of situations. The sports kit can be suggestive of dressing up as somebody else, an act undertaken to try and mask the problem that lies with the real self. This dressing up is crucially linked to story and structure, and plays a huge part in the depiction of genre. Sometimes in sports films a specific item of clothing will carry symbolic value, such as a cap or a pair of training shoes which hold meaning to the past, a person or a concept. Although this is part of the structural narrative of the film, it is an important part of the visual discourse of genre just as knives and masks are to the thriller. They too represent the situation of the characters, and when similarly used in other films of the genre, become a visual code or convention in themselves.

Elements of visual imagery are not ancillary components, however, merely inserted into a screenplay for quick-fix genre results. They may well come after the story, structure and character have been developed, but should be seen as a continuation of the same process. Although they are ways of 'dressing up' a narrative for visual consumption, they cannot dress up what is not already there. They come second to idea and plot in the writing process, but embody idea and plot in their existence. Objects and costumes emanate from the world of the story, and plot and scene design. We would warn screenwriters against simply adding what they think visually befits a genre, and instead let visual codes emerge from story, structure and character. In this way the screenplay will be tight, consistent, and most of all, true to itself.

7 Key Points and
Foundations Exercises

This final chapter illustrates key points covered in *Foundations*, and suggests exercises to develop a deeper understanding of them.

- **Subject: Ideas into Character**

Key point

Backstory is an essential tool in developing character. When exploring characters, asking personal questions will make them feel more real and rounded, and give the writer a stronger connection to them. The key to working with character is not to control them too much, but allow the writer's subconscious to come into play and get characters to 'talk'.

Exercise: Asking the right backstory questions

Rather than general exploration, it is often more effective to consider specific backstory questions with thematic relevance for the story. For instance, in a story where brother Angus and sister Julie are arguing over a family inheritance, *relevant* backstory questions to pose could be:

- What kind of relationship did they have when they were young?
- What do each of them think of their parents?
- What is their situation with money? How much do they need it and what for? What would happen if they did not have it?
- How do they feel about the family line? Are they close to their family or distant? Who in their family do they like and who do they dislike? Why?
- When was the first time Angus and Julie quarrelled as kids? Over what? What happened? Who won?
- What has the relationship dynamic been like in Julie and Angus' relationship as they grew up (teenagers, adults)?

- Who lives closest to home? What kind of relationships have they sustained with their family since leaving home?
- What has Angus never told Julie? What has Julie never told Angus?

To practice this approach, write a minimum of fifteen relevant backstory questions for each of these characters and situations:

(1) Jake, Pete and Sam work in the same office and are about to go on holiday together. At the last minute Sam drops out, making a weak excuse, leaving Jake and Pete in the lurch. Their friendship is tested as Pete gets drunk and goes to Sam's to have it out with him. Jake tries to restrain Pete but accidentally gets hit; he is badly injured and taken to hospital.
(2) Gwen has found a mystical stone in her back garden. Whenever she holds it, it seems to open a portal into a magical world full of monsters and moonshine. She is fascinated but terrified of it and tries to throw it away, but every morning it lies outside her back door, waiting for her.
(3) Henry has three daughters and two sons. His youngest is about to get married but Henry, disapproving of the wife-to-be, refuses to attend the wedding. The other children have tried persuading him but Henry will not budge.

Key point

The character arc is the journey a character travels from beginning to end of a story. All characters have arcs, not just protagonists. Useful 'maps' to character development, an arc can help writers isolate key story points and reveal relationship dynamics.

Exercise: Creating a character arc

Take all main characters in a story and ask the following of each:

- Where are they at the start?
- Where are they at the middle?
- Where are they at the end?

Think *emotionally*, *physically*, and around *status* or *power* issues. Look at the relationship between the character's want and need and how this changes. Try to locate the Central Dramatic Question or thematic issue in their arc. Do this for all major characters, then write out each character arc in brief form and compare them. What interesting relationships or character connections are revealed; what story moments present themselves; what thematic resonances make themselves known?

Key point

A story grows organically once the right protagonist is combined with the right antagonist(s), allowing thematically relevant conflict to emerge spontaneously. The function of the antagonist is to challenge the protagonist in a manner which forces the protagonist to face the issues that are essential to their arc. Therefore, antagonists are not just about creating conflict, but the *right kind* of conflict. Often the antagonist will have a similar objective to the protagonist, bringing them into maximum conflict, fighting for the same thing; they are thus a 'suitable opponent' by operating on a similar skill-level.

Exercise: Choosing the right antagonist

What kind of character would be a worthy antagonist to the protagonists below? Create at least five antagonists for each, making them as different as possible. For each antagonist, write out:

- Their main traits
- How they would create conflict for the protagonist
- What would happen between protagonist and antagonist when they meet

(1) ELLA is an eight-year-old who wants to win a dancing competition in her school, because she feels bullied and this is the only way she can prove to others what she is capable of.

(2) ARTHUR is seventy-two and in an old people's home. His family are far away and rarely visit. He had a good friend who recently died. Arthur loves horses and would love to go racing, but no one will take him. He dreams of riding across fields as he did in his youth.

(3) CHRISTINA is thirty-two and a mother of three. She divorced two years ago and would love to meet a new man, but is afraid of making changes.

- **Structure and Narrative**

Key Point

Stories built organically from character are often rich, solid and engaging, and if you explore your characters, stories tend to arise naturally. What emerges from a combination of characters may lead to a useful plot point or emotional situation, whether included in the script or not.

Exercise: Bringing people together

Pick two people you have observed or characters you have created, then put them together to see what happens. How do they push each other's buttons? What conflict ensues? What objectives do they share? Explore what *attracts* them to each other and what *repels* them, thinking of them as magnets: bringing together (*connection*) and pushing apart (*conflict*). Do this with different character combinations until you find engaging potential stories.

When there is an interesting relationship, introduce a *third* character into the mix and see what happens. Often *character triangles* create the strongest drama (not just love triangles but numerous tensions and character dynamics).

Key point

Whatever structure or genre you choose for a story, most forms emerge from basic-building blocks. This is not to restrict the narrative but rather to operate from a strong foundation from which mainstream or experimental narrative can radiate out. As the best story to tell may not always be obvious, building blocks also allow the writer to investigate an *idea* to determine whether it has enough fuel in the tank to become a *story*.

Exercise: Building the basics

Pick a new idea and use the checklist below to identify its essential story elements:

- Protagonist (who?)
- World (where?)
- Objective (what do they want?)
- Obstacle (what stands in their way?)

Create at least ten possible variations to mine the idea for maximum information before you settle on the one to tell. Try substituting different protagonists, different worlds, different problems, different objectives.

Key point

Stories are often discussed in terms of conflict, but an engaging story needs both *conflict* and *connection*: elements that cause problems and elements that make the audience care. Conflict is often created through the tension between *objective* and *obstacle*. The character's behaviour in dealing with obstacles gives the audience an insight into how much she wants to achieve her objective. With the idea of connection, the audience is shown why it is important the characters achieve their objective.

There are three types of story obstacle: self, others, and environment (physical world and ideological values). They can exist on a physical, mental or spiritual plane. The type of obstacles a character encounters determines what kind of arc and journey they experience, and what thematic resonances are created; it is therefore important to consider what the most relevant conflict for a story is.

Exercise: Creating conflict

Create a basic character: name, age, job.
Give them an objective: what they want or want to achieve.
Brainstorm at least twenty obstacles to this objective (use obstacles from all categories).

For instance, if fifty-year-old dinner lady Dora dreams of seeing the world, *possible obstacles* to her achieving this may be:

- She cannot afford it.
- She is terrified of flying.
- She buys a cruise ticket but the company goes bankrupt.
- She gets to Mexico but is kidnapped by terrorists.
- Her husband keeps her at home with emotional blackmail.
- She feels she is too old and should accept this as her life and be grateful.
- Her boss will not give her time off and if she goes, she will be fired.
- She cannot imagine leaving her nine cats that live indoors and depend on her.

- She is a terrible dreamer who cannot organise her way out of a paper bag.
- She cares for her elderly mother who lives with her.

Exercise: Creating connection

This exercise helps determine if a character's *motivation for their objective* is strong enough to carry the plot. Reversing the 'creating conflict' exercise, look again at Dora and find twenty reasons why she wants to see the world; why it matters to her and why it should matter to the audience. Another way to think about it is to consider what will happen if she fails to achieve her objective (*the stakes*).

Example *reasons why* Dora wants to see the world:

- She has spent all her life looking after others.
- She has never been anywhere beyond her little village.
- She only has six months to live.
- She has made a bet with her best friend who thinks she'll never do it.
- Her husband recently died and she is struggling with what to do with her life.
- She received a letter from an old flame who lives abroad who she never stopped thinking about.
- She has a secret map of a lost continent.
- She wants to prove to her explorer father she is not a mousey disappointment.
- She hates her life and dreams of the ocean even though she does not know why.

Once you have created a list for your own protagonist, look at which *motivation* fuels the character the most; which will keep them going the longest when the going gets tough. The key question to bear in mind is 'why will the audience care?' It is useful to undertake this exercise with all main characters in a story, both protagonists and antagonists, as it makes them rich and evenly matched, and allows more plot to emerge.

Key point

Different genres have different structural archetypes, as they aim to fulfil or address different audience expectations. Strong genre films are often about giving the audience what they want, but in a way they do not expect. To write a genre story, it is a good idea to study its arche-typal structure. One way to discover different narrative forms is to take the same premise and write it in different genres.

Exercise: Genre and structure

From one premise, create three different genres (sketch them out in basic tent pole form):

A large multinational organisation tries to buy out a small farm-ing community. When the community resists, the corporation reveals a darker side and resorts to very dirty tricks.

(1) Write it as a comedy (any sub-genre).
(2) Write it as a thriller (or horror).
(3) Write it as a love story (tragic or happy).

Read back the different versions and reflect on what this tells you about the relationship between genre and structure. How did having to create the story within a genre restrict or inspire you? How are the versions different or similar in story architecture, theme or protagonist arc? What is the relationship between protagonist arc, genre and structure?

- **Visual Storytelling**

Key point

Screenwriters have to find ways to externalise emotion so the audience understands the inner state of a character without having to explain it (*show, not tell*).

Exercise: Externalising emotion

Start with an emotion; pick your own or use one from the list below. Find at least ten ways to make it playable on screen through action, behaviour, event or image.

Loneliness
Love
Anger
Desperation

Fear
Curiosity
Insecurity
Sadness

As an example – Loneliness: A person…

- sitting apart from others as they laugh and talk.
- on their own in a huge desert.
- looking through a window at a party.
- clutching their dog.
- sitting on their own in an empty room, looking at old photographs.
- lying in bed staring straight ahead.
- lying in a large double bed with an empty space beside them.
- looking at dating ads in a magazine.
- trying to walk into a busy pub/disco/school but turning away.
- watching the telephone, waiting for it to ring.

Now try the exercise in reverse. Start by taking an action and write twenty different reasons why somebody might carry out this action. Prod as deeply and in as many varied directions as possible, and try to consciously change tone in every few items.

For instance, the action of someone 'being late' could happen because he/she:

- Missed the bus.
- Overslept.
- Got very drunk the night before.
- Has been engaged in frenetic sexual activity all morning.
- Is being bullied at work and is frightened of coming in.
- Got a phone call before they left to say their mother has died.
- Is always late because they are dippy and dreamy.
- Has got terrible toothache and has been waiting at the dentist for over two hours.
- Found a magic ring on the pavement and got transported to a faraway land.
- Found a wallet on the pavement and took it to the police, where they were mistaken for a murderer and held for questioning.
- Helped a crying child find its mother.
- Caused a terrible traffic accident.
- Sat in a café trying to build up the nerve to hand in their resignation.

Key point

To make scripts more *playable*, use verbs rather than adjectives. As verbs are action words, they allow events, rather than adjectives which are more passive. Specific verbs help screenwriters create effective, relevant scene description with one economical word.

Exercise: Verb hunt

Brainstorm at least fifteen synonyms for the common verb 'walk'. Stretch the verb in all possible directions with synonyms such as:

> *Saunter*
> *Skip*
> *Drag your feet*
> *Stumble*
> *March*

Now exchange the common verb ('walk') in the following sentence with one of the specific verbs from the list to see how it changes:

> *Betsy walks down the road.*

becomes:

> *Betsy saunters down the road.*
> *Betsy marches down the road.*
> *Betsy skips down the road.*

Consider what you know from the first sentence: *Betsy walks down the road*. Not much, we know what she is doing, but do not have a sense of why, how she feels about doing it, or how important it is to her. Now analyse the sentences with the specific verb and see what this tells you about how Betsy might be feeling, what kind of person she might be, or how important what she is doing is to her.

Key point

Objects are excellent tools in externalising emotion and internal dynamics. Adding an object to a scene can inform the audience how a character is feeling by the way they react to it or use it, and can show the status or balance of a relationship. An object might not have any intrinsic value, but should be carefully chosen to have symbolic or thematic resonance, to depict how relationships progress and situations change.

Exercise: Objects

Pick a scene from a film or TV drama you know well. Analyse all objects in a scene. Note how they help to reveal emotions, action, give relationship information, or any other ways they help the scene. Brainstorm other possible objects that could be used in this situation. What might belong in that location or to one of the characters? Come up with at least ten new objects and try them out to see how they help tell the story and show the characters' state of mind and relationship dynamics. Now go through your own script and underline or highlight all the objects you have used in your scene description.

Key point

Blocking is originally a directing term referring to the way characters relate to each other physically. There are three main areas: the character's relationship to *self*, to *others*, and to the *space*. Staging can both *complement* and *counterpoint* a scene (playing a love scene with characters far apart, unable to touch), but should always serve the story.

Exercise: Blocking and body language

Pick a scene from a film or TV drama you know well. Analyse how it uses character blocking and body language, then create at least five other possible ways you could make the characters relate to each other physically. How are they expressing their emotions or relationships through their bodies? Go through your own script and underline or highlight the blocking you have used. Can you explore it further to express the dynamics of a relationship, or express emotion and subtext in a more powerful, relevant way?

Key point

The environment (spaces and places) we put our characters in can have a huge impact on scenes. Not only does it create story information but also mood, geography and emotion.

Exercise: Environments

Pick three different scenes from a film or TV drama you know well. Analyse how they use their locations. For each, think of at least five other possible locations. Try to be as varied as you can, exploring unfamiliar and surprising options. How does each location change the scene? How does it affect the mood, scene moments, character dynamic, audience experience? Now go through your own script and write a list of all locations or environments you have used. Brainstorm at least five other possible locations for each of the scenes to see if you can improve upon dramatic possibilities and theme/tone. You may even find you want to shift the whole world of your story. This is useful to do at an early stage of an idea, as finding an unusual world can bring a whole new angle and freshness to a familiar story.

- **Dialogue and Voice**

Key point

Characters do not always listen and respond neatly. Instead, they have parallel conversations, interrupt, or don't listen. How characters interact with each other, how they listen and engage, what attention they give each other, all speaks volumes about the state of their relationship.

Exercise: Cross talk

Pick a scene from one of your scripts. Try rewriting it by making one or both characters interrupt each other, have parallel conversations, be silent or not listen. This can work both in a positive (e.g. creating excitement) or negative sense (e.g. conflict). See what happens to the relationship dynamic and feel of the scene when the dialogue and emotional exchange changes. What do you discover about the subtext of the scene? Do you find new ways to make the scene flow that feel relevant to theme, tone and genre? What do you feel about the scene as an emotional exchange between the characters and the dynamic of their relationship?

Key point

It is not only the words that characters speak that are important, but their underlying meaning (*subtext*). Dialogue is not only content, but an exchange between characters where communication takes place on a number of levels.

Exercise: Saying everything with nothing

Write a scene with two or three characters, where the characters seem to be talking about nothing but the price of potatoes. However, what they are saying below the surface is completely different. There are three different contexts to attempt:

Love Declaration

The characters talk about the price of potatoes, but are in fact really discussing how they feel about each other and how much they secretly love each other. Maybe one finds it harder than the other to express how they feel? Maybe both are shy or nervous?

Thriller Threat

Characters talk about the price of potatoes, but in fact are suggesting one is in imminent danger of being killed if he does not start behaving. They could be speaking in code, or in the language of the world they inhabit (the fact that a very real danger is spoken about obliquely or calmly can make it much more frightening, so it can be a good exercise in using counterpoint and contrast to create meaning through subtext).

Comedy Secret

Characters talk about the price of potatoes, but are in fact referring to a secret that two of them have which they cannot reveal in front of the third. How is one going to make the second understand what she is trying to say when she cannot state it openly? Is the other person constantly misunderstanding, or do they indeed understand, but then add a complication the first had not thought of? Making it hard for characters is often useful for comedy as we witness them struggling to find a way to deal with the situation.

Part II

Speculations

8   Exploring   Possibilities

Critical appraisal of screenwriting is an emerging discipline. Theories and discussions available to screenwriting have their own unique position, concerned with practice as opposed to solely 'post event' analysis. Knowledge can be created and relocated in an attempt to contextualise screenwriting as a process, and screenwriters as practitioners: before writing (ideas gathering, inspiration, character development), during writing (screenplay drafting) and after writing (editing, viewing, reflecting). It is the intention of this *Speculations* section to highlight unusual practices, innovative approaches, and critical reflections, which are either culturally evolving or already exist but often go unexamined in standard screenwriting training. By revisiting similar territories as in *Foundations* but from a different perspective, the aim here is to challenge and stimulate practitioners and theoreticians to venture beyond the familiar, whether in process or product; to look beneath the surface of screenwriting and explore its concepts more deeply. Screenwriters do not always have to accept the current status quo in the industry, but can explore other constantly evolving avenues. It is our aim that *Speculations* will boost your ideas and confidence to help take craft, creativity and career into your own hands and to consciously engage with satisfying creative practices.

Working with others

As discussed in Chapter 12, notions of authorship in screenwriting are complex and continually evolving. Writers often consider an idea their own, and novice writers are notoriously concerned about copyright. With more experience it becomes clear that the sourcing and shaping of scripts is a fluid, flexible process. Chapter 6 refers to the deeply collaborative nature of screenwriting, and how writers must be able to work with feedback. It is therefore imperative that screenwriters examine current and possible opportunities in working with others, and how to fulfil such practices in creative, productive ways.

It is not always possible to pinpoint where an idea comes from; it may start with a general note of dissatisfaction from a producer, which inspires the writer to create a character, which a script editor helps shape. In development meetings and writers' groups, good ideas regularly come from many different minds. What the writer does is decide which ideas fit with the story and oversees the overall shape. Screenwriting thus challenges the notion that a piece of creative writing is purely the work of a single author. Instead, it allows room for the creative process to breathe, and the story rather than the author becomes key. Indeed, one could argue that the screenwriter is the *director of the text*, the one that brings focus and cohesion, rather than the sole *creator of the text*. Of course the majority of script and story material will (and should) come from the writer, but what this concept emphasises is the importance of the collaborative process, whether formally stated or not, and reframes the writer's role within it. This may seem to further undermine the status of the writer within the script industry, but we would rather argue that it opens up the process and puts the writer at the centre of it, recognising the practices that are already in place and reclaiming the importance of the writer within them.

This chapter examines various ways of working with others, from 'invisible' collaborations such as receiving feedback and working with a script editor, both crucial in current industry practice but rarely discussed when training screenwriters; to more innovative possibilities such as team development, working with actors and interactive technology. We would thus like to question the hegemony both of current working practices and the notion of the single author as key to a successful text.

Working with feedback

Though the screenwriting process is filled with a flow of constant feedback, it is rare that it is discussed as a working practice and examined in terms of the skills needed to negotiate it successfully, both in terms of creating a strong script and a strong working relationship with people a writer may need to nurture for future commissions. Working with feedback can be confusing and precarious, full of pitfalls and time wasting, and it is important the writer knows how to receive and apply feedback. Commonly referred to as script notes, feedback comes from a variety of sources – directors, producers, executives, actors, script editors – and can often be conflicting or lack focus. As Hollywood writer Terry Rossio (of screenwriting duo Ted & Terry) details:

> You are always co-writing the script with somebody and the sooner you scope out who that is, and figure out their take on the material, the better off you will be. Could be the director, could be the development executive, could be the studio head. But somebody in power at some point is going to tell you what you can, and cannot, write.
>
> (1997: 7)

It is thus the job of the writer to sift through notes and distil the bigger picture, asking:

- What are the essential points that need to be addressed?
- What are the real problems behind the comments?
- How to address all wishes without losing focus or compromising the project?
- How to move the project forward in a satisfying and relevant way?

Inexperienced writers can sometimes feel personally attacked by feedback, and become defensive or dejected. It is worth remembering that in a script meeting everyone in the room usually shares the same goal – to improve the story – and this is what matters rather than personal egos. However, sometimes it becomes clear the writer and producer's view of the script are very different and this may mean the working relationship is no longer viable. Most of the time however, problems and conflicts are there to be worked through, and it is important for the writer to show they are capable of receiving script notes and acting upon them creatively. That said, the writer also has to learn not to accept comments wholesale. There may be many useful, interesting ideas but not all of them will serve the script. Therefore, writers have to learn the skill of *filtering feedback*, testing it against their own notions, making sure the script is not diluted by changes made for the sake of it or because they feel fresher than what already exists.

Working with and developing a story is a constant balance between opening up and closing down. On the one hand, writers have to listen to comments, accept constructive criticism and be brutally honest about story problems. On the other, they simultaneously have to keep in mind the focus and essence, how to keep it coherent, what the key issues are, and what is unproductive to compromise on. A successful writer is one who can balance these two aspects and find a way to apply sometimes conflicting, complex and unclear feedback in the most relevant and productive manner.

All producers are not expert story analysts, and may flag up a symptom without correctly identifying the underlying cause. In such cases the writer must clarify the problem the producer is subconsciously detecting and decide what issue really needs attention. Without such astute analysis, a script can quickly be dismantled and weakened, and it is the writer's duty to keep it on track. If there are uncertainties, the writer should ask questions to clarify the producer's narrative aims to make sure they are delivering what has been asked for. This increases the chances of finding creatively satisfying ways to shape a story, instead of becoming embroiled in an escalating war of words. As the producer is nearly always the person who hires or fires the writer, it is crucial to understand how to work well together, why they demand certain changes, and how they think about screen stories. Becoming familiar with the basics of film financing, sales and distribution gives valuable insights into the producer's world and helps writers understand their point of view. Another potential source of help is the script editor.

The role of the script editor

A script editor is usually hired by a producer (occasionally a writer) to help develop the script. The script editor understands the producer's wishes and brief, and it is their duty to nurture the writer and script through the process and ensure that the producer receives the draft they have asked for. However, in script editing training – which tends to be informal and on the job – there is a focus mainly on script analysis and less on working process. We would argue that the duty of a script editor is actually twofold: first, to ensure good quality development of the story in the appropriate direction, and secondly, to understand the writer's working method and best support him/her through this. Some writers need a lot of handholding, some work better with a loose reign. A good script editor should understand how to get the best out of a writer and tailor-make a development process which allows the best script to be forged. This way the producer will obtain value for money and the writer will feel confident and satisfied with their work. Addressing the psychology of script editing is thus an important but often overlooked part of the development process. As Andermatt suggests:

> It is not enough for a script editor to have technical skills, to know the 'rules'. What she or he needs most of all is a feeling for other people.

> The very first thing a script editor needs to achieve, before getting too deep into the script, is to gain the confidence of the people involved. Empathy, this word so often used in order to define the ideal link between the audience and the characters, also has to be applied to the relationship between the script editor and the writer.
>
> (2003: 53)

Instead of telling a writer what to do, or offering straight solutions, a more constructive script editing approach is to ask questions: what is the purpose of a plot point, what is the story really about, what does a character want, why do they take action? This stimulates the writer to find their own answers, leading to a more cohesive and robust script. The writer is the writer after all, and the script editor is there to offer support, inspiration and clarity. A crucial discipline of script editing is the need to focus on what the producer and writer wish to create, and act as mediator between them, rather than involve personal taste. Instead of entering the territory as co-writer, the script editor provides perspective, acting as *the writer's mirror*, asking questions and reflecting the real state of the story so the writer can see it clearly and find their own path through it. This necessitates that the script editor discovers and really hears what both writer and producer wish for and helps bring them together in order for one story to be told.

The key duty of the script editor in film is to negotiate the producer's brief, diagnose the real reasons for story problems and help structure the development process. This is why it can be useful for writers to work as script editors, as it constantly hones script analysis skills in how to locate and solve problems and make the development process more productive. Many writers do not have enough understanding of how to approach rewriting, and rather than attempting to deal with everything at once or attacking weaknesses in a random order, good script editing offers effective action plans for the writer in how to structure the next draft, highlighting the primary story issues that need addressing and suggesting the order in which to do so. Since a recurring and substantial problem in scripting is 'story fatigue' (where the writer loses interest and passion in the story), informed and productive ways of working through development is crucial to keeping a writer inspired and producing the best work right to the end. This is where a good script editor can make all the difference and there is no reason to work without one, as this kind of creative collaboration – a creative mirror – is key to quality work.

In television drama the script editor works somewhat differently, their function being more practical, keeping writers organised to deadlines, offering instruction on what ideas are possible and relevant within the format, and ensuring a coherent series 'voice' when episodes are created by different writers. Multiple writers contributing to one world is common in television since the faster pace necessitates having a number of writers to deliver on time, but rather than just a solution to an organisational problem, we would suggest this is also a potential hive of creativity, with many possible rewards.

Team development and co-writing

Though rarely discussed in most screenwriting literature, *team development* is relatively common in US television writing, particularly in sitcoms and comedy series such as *The Simpsons*, *Friends*, *Sex and the City* and *Ugly Betty*. It is widely acknowledged that a 'family' of writers and development personnel who know and trust each other can work together in a hothouse atmosphere and raise the standard of the work. Plot lines, twists, jokes and character arcs are developed by working together in story conferences, as writers inspire each other and smooth out problems before they reach the page. There are potential pitfalls with such approaches but in professional practice team development is generally led by a producer, script editor or lead writer (*showrunner*) who works with writers used to sharing ideas and collaborating creatively.

In the UK, this is a rare working practice (exceptions include *My Family* and *After You've Gone*),[1] partly because it has not historically been a tradition and often because there is not enough money. Mal Young, ex-BBC Controller of Continuing Series, argues:

> because [UK] television is based on the theatre and radio, it's much more about the authored voice...So we've never really empowered writers to become showrunners. We tend to say, you're writers and they are the producers and the two should never really mix.
>
> (quoted in Marlow, 2003: 17)

Team development does exist to some degree on soap operas, where staff writers meet for story conferences to brainstorm future storylines. Indeed, during the early 1990s Mal Young, as producer of groundbreaking UK soap *Brookside*, applied a development system which series creator Phil Redmond had encountered in the USA:

> Once a month we'd have a two-day storylining meeting and it was like chairing an amazing creative machine...[the writers] had real

ownership...Each writer still writes their piece on their own, but then they come together as a group and help each other resolve any problems. It's fantastically liberating because you have four great, creative heads.

(Ibid.: 19)

Although some producers have adopted aspects of team development for drama series, such as Shed Productions' *Bad Girls* and *Footballers' Wives*, it is rare as a regular feature in the UK. Instead, writers work on individual episodes with a script editor, rarely meeting other series writers to exchange and polish ideas. Nevertheless, as discussed in the case studies below, there is nothing to stop writers from creating their own team development to experiment with less traditional working practices. It is a useful discipline to try as it moves writers away from purist notions of authorship into a more communal atmosphere where they may find creative skills improving dramatically. Chapter 14 offers a complementary exercise in this.

Co-writing is a more constrained version of team development, where two writers work as a unit. As in team development, it allows writers to spark off each other but as with traditional writing, it produces one script. The process can be approached in a variety of ways, with pitfalls as well as rewards. In the UK co-writing is commonly found in television sitcom or comedy writing (*Marks & Gran, Galton & Simpson*), whereas in the US it is not uncommon in feature film (*Elliot & Rossio, Ganz & Mandel, Kurtzman & Orci*). Some co-writing partnerships are so successful that their work becomes a 'brand', mainly for industry but sometimes for audiences, creating one voice from two writers: 'Dick Clement and Ian La Frenais are as inextricably connected as Lennon and McCartney, perhaps more so. My otherwise hair-splitting Penguin TV Companion makes do with one entry for the two of them' (Anon, 2002: para 1). Like well-established screenwriting auteurs (see Chapter 12), these co-writers become renowned for their joint voice. They have such a strong and successful working bond it would be difficult to see them working apart, and they themselves may share this dilemma as they rely upon each other to fuel the creative juices. Other writers co-work with different collaborators, such as Graham Linehan, who wrote surreal UK sitcom *Father Ted* with Arthur Mathews and *Black Books* with actor Dylan Moran, as well as material for comedy shows such as *The Fast Show*.

In terms of actual creative process, some co-writers such as Clement & La Frenais (*Auf Wiedersehen Pet, Porridge, Whatever*

Happened to the Likely Lads?) work literally side by side; others do their own drafting then exchange work. Whichever method is employed, there are important issues to consider when embarking on a co-writing project. What is the relationship between the writers; what makes the partnership stronger than individual writing? When co-writing occurs because of financial or practical reasons it can be weak or problematic. What tends to work better is if the writers know (consciously or sub-consciously) how they complement each other: one may be stronger on character and dialogue, the other at visual storytelling and structure. There may be excellent chemistry to inspire each other, or share a passion and knowledge for a certain genre. Douglas's comments on team development fit just as well with co-writing: 'the act of creativity is not private…Writers tend to want to work with other writers who enable them to do their best work… choosing collaborators who make them comfortable enough to take creative risks' (2007: 168).

Whatever the reason for the partnership, it is essential it becomes more than the sum of its parts; that both writers agree on working practices and the essence of the story. If writers are to write together, they need to ensure they are really writing the same script. This sounds obvious but it is alarming how often writers (or writers and producers) assume this is the case without discussing it. Done right, co-writing can be highly exciting and invigorating, a challenging and enlightening practice to engage with, if only as an exercise.

Below are two case studies examining how unusual collaborative practices can enhance creativity and challenge received notions of authorship. Rather than adopt the hierarchical structure of team development, where writers work according to the directions of the show-runner, these examples demonstrate what is possible in independent arenas where collaboration can be more democratic and experimental.

Interactive screenwriting (Craig Batty)

The Internet is producing a wealth of opportunities for screenwriters, both professional and amateur. Not only have technological advancements dissolved space, time and place, they have facilitated opportunities for personal participation in a world of writing: projects, competitions, networking, feedback, training. Never before have aspiring and professional screenwriters been able to congregate with like-minded people with such ease and breadth. Websites such as Shooting People, BBC Writersroom and Zoetrope are designed by and for those

with experiences in screenwriting, sharing information and opportunities to help people fulfil their ambitions in a collaborative 'digital'
community. The World Wide Web has certainly enabled worldwide
writing, as in the case of sixty6 films' online initiated feature, *Dogberry
and Bob: Private Investigators*. Taking place over a period of almost two
years (2005–7), the project saw the development and production of a
feature film utilising the Internet to source talent and crew and, more
importantly, to develop and write the script via an online writing community. This is a key example of how traditional film-making processes
can be challenged, offering non-elitist, personally driven avenues for
exploration and experimentation. In this case, writers and creative
thinkers from the UK and Europe offered ideas and snatches of script
to push along the writing process from the very launch of the project.
One of the creators and directors, Warren Dudley, explains in an interview with me the reason for this interactive initiative:

> We had recently made a comedy pilot called *Slightly Better Homes*, a
> spoof of Channel 4's *Selling Houses*, and had the idea of producing a
> series online an episode at a time with the public choosing the next
> episode etc. This morphed into the idea of the feature film...We hoped
> that giving the project an interactive edge would help build up a higher
> level of interest than producing the film traditionally. Kind of giving us
> a *Dogberry and Bob* fan base before anyone had even seen the movie.

Dudley and co-creator/director Roger O'Hara had already set-up aptly
named website, www.yourmovie.co.uk, which positioned the *Dogberry
and Bob* community's involvement with the development of the film.
The website was used as an interface between creators and contributors, 'advertising' every week or two the new material that was being
sought to add to the screenplay, and at the same time, showcasing some
of the scenes and ideas that had been supplied. This level of engagement,
typified by the use of discussion boards for peer feedback, demonstrates
how those with ambitions to be involved in a filmmaking project can
cut their teeth by experimenting in a safe environment, and how creative collaboration can enhance the results of an individual. Because
the project was not responsible to a corporate machine, and because it
was fluid in its ability to use or reject ideas, it was a safe way for aspiring writers (and later production crew) to play around with ideas and
receive unprejudiced yet highly useful feedback about their work.

   I was involved in the project as script editor, taken on board to work
with the masses of material submitted and incorporated into the screenplay, ensuring consistency in voice and vision. In many ways this is

a traditional way of working, taking an objective, critical view of the writing while at the same time trying not to stifle the writer's creativity, but the difference with this project was that there were many writers and their work was borne out of interactive involvement. The script editing role was therefore somewhat different to usual practice. Reading sections at a time which were an amalgamation of the creators' vision with the contributors' ideas and idiosyncrasies, the screenplay literally screamed with a dozen voices which needed to be carefully orchestrated. The overall story and structure was perhaps the easy part, the creators having a clear idea of how the plot would develop to tell the story. What was more difficult, and a direct result of its collaborative, interactive nature, was honing dialogue and ensuring flow of voice. From draft to draft as new material was added, it became apparent that jokes and scenes could work well on their own but did not befit the whole. The method for editing the work became the active incorporation of ideas and concepts, mainly put together at the creators' end, yet sustaining an established 'voice' by toothcomb editing of dialogue and scene action. Usually a writer is given notes and guidance as to how to progress to the next draft themselves; but because this was a collaborative, 'remote' project, input from script editor and creators was paramount. This brings into question notions of authorship and project control, asking whether the interactive contributors would ever have equal status in the hierarchical flow. Nevertheless, writers were never cheated of their work and had a major influence in the screenplay's development. As Dudley commented:

> The work sent in certainly gave us plenty of thoughts about our lead characters' traits and quirks. A few little sayings that cropped up became a big part of what we were trying to achieve. What really struck me about the whole collaborative process is how much time and effort people are prepared to put in to something that to them is just an interesting internet project … this gave us a little push whenever we were struggling a bit – a real need to give these talented people something back that they would be proud to say they were part of.

The *Dogberry and Bob* project demonstrates how we can speculate upon the changing nature of screenwriting practice. Firstly, not only did the originators have a means of producing a film but the project's Internet-based development method meant many people who might not have had such an opportunity found themselves working on something real. The potential of the Internet to allow participation in projects traditionally conceived and executed by few is none more evident than with this. The way in which the screenplay was formed also offers useful insights into alternative methods of development. From initial storylining to eventual writing, professionals learned from amateurs and amateurs learned from professionals. Although in some ways it was the professionals who directed the screenplay and had final say about words on pages, it could not have been achieved without the commitment of aspiring professionals. The project facilitated a process whereby ideas were thrown into the pot, and though filtered and shaped by those with more experience, such ideas encompassed visions of people who, ostensibly, represent the audience. Screenwriting may benefit from this notion in wider terms in order for 'real voices' to be heard. Although there are limitations on the material used, perhaps professional screenwriters could be more open to this idea in order that they create dramas that not only speak to the audience, but also speak of the audience. This would be a difficult feat to achieve in many conventional productions, but with the explosion of digital broadcasting and proliferation in niche-channelling, maybe there is room for further, more conscious experimentation.

Story from character: Working with actors (Zara Waldeback)

Another form of creative collaboration is where writers develop story with actors. This method has been used by writer–directors such as Mike Leigh, where actors build on his ideas through improvising character. Here we suggest a related but different practice, based on directing methods adapted to work for screenwriting purposes, for use by writers.

Traditionally, screenwriters and actors tend to meet mainly for the script read-through, an opportunity to hear dialogue and give it final polish. However, writers can involve actors much earlier in the process to explore character and build story. This can prove a very fruitful combination: actors bring a deep understanding of character motivation, subtext and relationship dynamics – essentially *the moment*; writers bring a sense of finding structure, direction and connection of these, essentially *momentum*. Writers can find great inspiration and depth from working with actors, not only in the formal manner of creating story, but also by exploring already existing characters and relationships to test the credibility of arcs, scene writing and theme.

A project exploring the possibilities of writer–actor collaborations was set-up using UK-founded website Shooting People, originally created to enable grass roots networking in filmmaking and screenwriting communities. A director collected ten actors and four writers (found through Shooting People) to create short scripts. Each actor was asked to bring a character of their own creation and attend the first workshop in character. The writers simply had to attend, observe and pay attention. Every actor performed a monologue as the writers watched, then the writers suggested potential character pairings to test and establish relationships, mainly through family, work or romance contexts. The writers spent a few days deepening these pairs and situations, offering them back to the actors as improvisations, where again the writers watched closely, offering suggestions on how to develop or expand a situation. In this way, numerous stories began to take shape, growing slowly and organically from character, themes, objectives and obstacles, and the writers' main work was not so much to create original material as create connections between characters. At the end of the workshop period, the writers picked the emerging stories they were most drawn to, and crafted complete short scripts from them. Some moments and dialogue from the improvisations were used, but mainly the scripts were original material from the writers based on and inspired by what the actors and writers had shaped together.

In this, writers and actors can be seen to collaborate closely in a process that allows a deep sculpting of story from a set of originally unrelated characters, through leaping into the creative waters of improvisation. Such brainstorming demands a certain amount of faith, opening and trusting that something will unfold, but a level of technique is also needed to make it fruitful. Most writers (and a surprising number of directors) have little understanding of working with actors or how to structure improvisation and it is important to learn the essentials. Paradoxically, although improvisation is in its nature free-form, it is most productive when given clear boundaries, particularly a *situation* ('a couple view a flat'), a clear *objective* ('Mary wants more space; Diana wants to punish her for last night's argument') and an *ending* ('the viewing is over'). With these guidelines, actors can embrace the improvisation and provide relevant and useful material. It is the writer's task to guide actors into the territory they want to explore and with such preparatory work comes the added bonus of writers naturally focusing and digging deeper. Working with actors can thus explore existing story problems as well as create new storylines. Having to face characters and relationships in concrete physical form can help writers untie plot knots, deepen relationships, even experiment with structure. Exploring character with actors who have to be clear on their motivation and behaviour, forces writers to face problems they may otherwise sweep under the carpet. It can be a highly useful part of development, even if a script is created in an otherwise conventional manner. Judith Weston's book *Directing Actors* (1996) gives further advice on working with actors, and though aimed at directors, is written with regard to the screen and much can be applied to the writer–actor relationship.

9 Subjects: Ideas into Characters

In *Foundations*, Chapter 2 discusses the importance of character and its close relation to story, and how to develop ideas using concepts such as objectives, power questions and arcs. This chapter offers further ways of thinking about ideas, not only how to have them but how to develop them; using existing techniques in innovative ways, looking more deeply at the relation of story and form, exploring a different approach to character and balancing on the boundary between fiction and the real. All these creative territories share an intention to broaden the writer's creative spectrum, and ask critical questions of the assumed notions of creativity and storytelling in current screenwriting practice.

Sourcing ideas for the screen

Within traditional screenwriting training there is a lack of focus on creativity and a tendency to approach it from a 'mechanical' viewpoint (see Chapters 2 and 13). In fact, much craft and creativity is needed when sourcing ideas, and it is important for writers to acknowledge that their job is not just to type script pages but to expand their creative territory, daydream, observe situations, explore human psychology and allow time for an idea to breathe, percolate and simmer. The life of a writer is not simply to write but to create space for stories to emerge, and at all times be ready to be inspired.

Writers are often faced with the clichéd question 'where do you get your ideas?' In working with screenwriters and students, time and again we have witnessed the birthing of ideas and there is never one size that fits all. What is of more concern is when there seems no discipline applied to the creation process. Often writers settle into development with the first idea that comes without considering whether it is suitable for the screen or the best idea to write at this point. Mainly this comes down to a lack of understanding of the industry (see Chapter 6) or an inability to trust and spend time on idea creation. The uninitiated often consider the creation of ideas as something mystical, whereas writers know it is simply down to practice. As Natalie Goldberg argues: 'It is odd that we never question the feasibility of a football team practising long hours for one game; yet in writing we rarely give ourselves the space for practice' (1986: 11). This tends to be particularly true of screenwriters, who often have less exposure to free-standing writing exercises than those trained in fiction or poetry. Creative thinking and idea manufacturing is not something writers have to wait around for until inspiration strikes; they are skills that can be trained and honed as much as character work or visual storytelling. Nervous novices unused to the creative process sometimes see creativity as a 'bucket' instead of a 'tap' – the more ideas they scoop out, the fewer there will be left. However, when viewing it as a tap – the more you turn on, the more will come out – then with practice and awareness there will be an unceasing flow of ideas.

So how to turn on the tap? There are many excellent creative writing books to help tune up creative muscles, but unfortunately in screenwriting literature this is seldom addressed. This has resulted in the industry receiving a large proportion of well written but rather unexciting scripts, and so they turn to fiction writers, playwrights, even documentary makers to find ideas with more fire. In *Making a Good Writer Great*, Linda Seger suggests that 'creativity comes from a collision of ideas not ordinarily thought of as fitting together' (1999: 8) and her book is one of the few within the screenwriting canon that actively address the creative process. Thus one way to become more creative is to create unusual combinations, and other techniques include:

- *Keeping a scrapbook* – ideas often arrive unfinished so it is a good practice to keep a scrapbook with anything that feels inspiring or interesting: newspaper stories, images, poems, overheard conversations, dreams, phrases, words or titles. This raw material can be dipped into whenever a dose of inspiration is needed.
- *Writer's journal* – writing regular pages of free association in order to empty the mind and tune into emotions. A way of limbering up and clearing out to prepare for the working day, it can also pay unexpected dividends in ideas and character.
- *Observing people and situations* – daily life is an endless source of ideas, inspiration and detail and can be used to help develop a particular idea or as general awareness practice.

- *Using opposites* – as the brain tends to get locked into similar well-worn grooves, opposites are an excellent method of jolting thinking down fresh unexpected pathways.
- *Brainstorming, lists and free association* – classic ways of allowing uncontrolled expression, often leading to interesting surprises or ways to unblock stuckness.
- *Creative writing exercises* – there are a huge number of creative writing exercises in fiction writing books, and it is useful to attempt at least a couple every week.
- *Using images or visual aids* – sometimes it can be better to bypass words and allow pictures to create inspiration. Cut out images that appeal, then combine them in interesting ways to see what happens; do stories or characters emerge?

It can also be useful for screenwriters to attend fiction writing classes as this field of study has a longer history of exploring and engaging with creative techniques. What is important is to train in skills before problems such as writer's block arise, and every screenwriter should take time to practice regularly. Creativity exercises can help during many different phases of the process, to sharpen-up technique and strengthen confidence, as well as make writers more aware and help them interact with the world as a writer should; attentive and curious, constantly looking, listening and feeling. It is crucial for screenwriters wishing to sustain a career to think about creativity as well as craft, and actively train themselves in this. Inspiration does not just strike, it can be summoned at will if one is prepared to work for it, and Chapter 14 offers a selection of exercises.

Pitching as telling vs pitching as selling

Another way to explore and expand ideas is to work with pitching techniques, to test the narrative possibilities dormant inside the 'story seed'. Pitching is a staple of every screenwriter's life. It is as important to sell work as it is to write it, and *pitching as selling* is the traditional form whereby a writer summarises their idea to a producer or financier. This can be done in a formal setting such as a proposal document or funding meeting, or through informal channels such as a party – writers have to be prepared to pitch at any time. The main purpose is to get the reader or listener to want to know more, usually by asking to see the script or treatment. It is therefore important to give only as much information as will whet and not satiate the appetite. The most common problem when pitching in person is telling too much, making the listener confused, bored or both. A more effective approach is to outline basic story elements then let a conversation develop, allowing the listener to ask questions and become engaged in the story. There are different pitching styles and writers do not always know what producers will be looking for, so preparation is key to clarify the dramatic essentials:

- a protagonist with an objective
- a situation with something at stake
- the main problem, usually an antagonist or series of obstacles

With these elements in place, the pitch should have power and clarity. If there are problems or weaknesses in these basic areas, they are worth addressing before going further. In every premise, it is crucial to know the beginning, middle and end, and useful to give a sense of genre, world and theme. This 'recipe' is all a pitch needs: clear strong essential information, without attempting convoluted plotting. It is also crucial to pitch in the *tone* of the script: comedies pitches have to be funny, thrillers or horrors full of suspense, dramas full of emotion. 'Show, don't tell' applies as much to pitching as it does to scriptwriting. Producers, executives and financiers have heard thousands of pitches and know what to look for in order to make a decision, so offer brief clear essentials and let them ask about the rest. This will make the writer appear professional and if the premise is not to the producer's taste, they can ask for other ideas (another golden rule – always bring more than one idea).

Selling an idea, however, is not the only function of pitching. Instead, *pitching as telling* can help refine ideas, find clarity and focus and test the market. Here writers use the pitch as a tool to discover what is working in the story, if it has potential, or to try a number of ideas to decide which is worth developing. By presenting the story succinctly, the writer can test its essence: what is the core, what is its potential, can it withstand a long and arduous development process? By telling the story in miniature via a pitch, the writer begins to hear it speak, and gets a sense of what kind of story it could become.

Pitching as telling thus allows a writer to delve deeply into an idea very quickly, without spending time on outlines. It is an efficient method to explore which idea feels most promising and which falls apart under scrutiny, as well as gain a sense of how to develop it. It is interesting to see which ideas naturally begin to grow; which stick in the mind even though they may be troublesome. Crucially perhaps, which idea does the writer keep wanting to tell? A writer has to find something to love in every idea (even if it is not their own source material), otherwise it is difficult to live with it during the many months of development. There are pitfalls with the pitching as telling method as some ideas sound better as a pitch than others, and just because there is no strong way to pitch an idea, it does not necessarily mean it cannot work. In this case, try to find out why the pitch is failing. Is it because the writer needs to refine their pitching skills, or because they have not spent enough time exploring the premise? Is there something that is being avoided? Is the idea not sitting easily within the screenwriting medium?

As a working practice, pitching as telling is an important tool in building an initial relationship between writer and story, and can help writers generate story, evaluate ideas, build a portfolio of future work, and explore their voice, all without developing long documents. Time spent on pitching as telling can be hugely worthwhile, as it requires writers to choose projects worth developing with awareness and commitment.

Ideas and form: Narrative possibilities in the short film

One of the key aspects of developing ideas is to understand the form that most suits a premise. Some ideas naturally fit into a feature or television series, some are clearly novels or plays, some have an ability to be adapted across forms. When choosing to develop an idea into a story, it is important to consider the challenges and potential within the combination of form and idea. Some writers find they are more naturally drawn to one form over another, such as sitcom, children's drama or certain genre features. It can be an excellent practice to occasionally try a new or more unfamiliar form as this forces a writer's creative thinking to take new paths and allows freshness in. One way of accomplishing this is to experiment with short scripts. Unlike television and feature film scripts, the short form allows for a wide range of ideas. This is partly due to the fact that it is less business-driven and, like the short story in comparison to the novel, functions both as story in miniature and on its own terms. Short scripts are a rich area that can contain far more experimentation than features or TV writing, and challenge conventional notions of what constitutes a screen narrative, opening doors to possible innovation and application of such ideas to longer formats.

Many writers approach the short script as a condensed version of classical three act narrative: a character wants something, they try to achieve it but encounter obstacles until they finally manage to reach some kind of resolution. This can be a very useful method as it allows novice writers to practice classical narrative technique and provide solid foundation to their craft. A short script is brief enough to allow a complete narrative, without too much material to manage. In this way the short is an excellent form for writers to learn their craft, and certainly worth attempting many times before tackling a larger piece. The brevity of the format also challenges writers to be economical with scene writing. Many try to fit too much story into a short form whereas the idea needs to be contained enough to follow a satisfactory journey in 5–10 minutes (some years ago, a short film was often 15–20 minutes, but today festivals and funders tend to seek a shorter short of ten minutes or under, and in some cases such as the *Brief Encounter* festival's 'Depict!' scheme, only ninety seconds. See www.depict.org).

A short that successfully follows a classical narrative in a way that works with rather than against the brevity of the short form is *The Fishmonger*. The script was commissioned for UK production as part of the Orange FilmFour Prize for Short Film, and is an almost perfect three act story in miniature. In a sleepy fishing town the local fishmonger goes happily about his business until a new, modern upstart suitably named Mr Leech arrives (inciting incident). Not only does Mr Leech wear a white coat and ponytail, he also drives a van as opposed to the fishmonger's traditional cart. The fishmonger realises his way of life is under threat as the local fishermen are happy to provide Mr Leech with the fish the fishmonger had previously thought of as his (end of Act 1). A fierce competition breaks out between the two as they race to the harbour each morning to be the first to collect the treasured fish. Every day the balance tips as they try harder and harder to win (Act 2), until one day Mr Leech – accidentally on purpose? – knocks the fishmonger into the sea (end of Act 2, lowest point). As the fishmonger flails around underwater (biggest battle), he is overcome with the beauty of the sea, and literally sees the light. He decides to give up fishmongering and turns his shop into an oversized aquarium (hardest choice). The venture is a huge success and he feels harmoniously happy in the world, with Mr Leech forced to concede (resolution). What makes this script even more powerful is the fact that such a clear and entertaining story is told with only one or two lines of dialogue, and is an excellent example of visual storytelling, all in under five minutes.

However, the short offers far more than miniature features, and many writers embrace the opportunity of crafting an unconventional narrative and exploring the many creative shapes the compact form allows. Not driven by sales and commercialism, in many ways it is the script form closest to art and poetry, with a variety of expressive possibilities. *When I Was Falling ...* (winner of Depict!, 1999) is a ninety-second story of the highly dramatic set against the mundane. As a man jumps to his death from the top of a building, the camera moves in to glimpse the lives behind the windows he falls past. Inside nothing much happens; outside the drama of death unfolds unseen. Told without dialogue, it is a powerful visual poem, and though it has a contained and clear character arc (beginning with the man jumping and ending with him hitting the ground), there is no sense of character motivation or obstacles, but rather a focus on theme, atmosphere and subtext that is resonant of poetic metaphor and structure.

Telling Lies is a short that focuses its dramatic conflict on the relationship between sound and image. With no visual element beyond playfully expressive graphic text on a black screen, the story unfolds mainly through dialogue in a series of telephone conversations. As a young man is awoken after a drunken night out he gradually recollects, and is confronted by, the unsavoury events of the night before. What makes the storytelling so effective, beyond its brilliant simplicity and pure use of form, is that during the audio conversations, text on screen allows privileged access to the man's inner thoughts, creating a deft, satirical and hilarious situation that speaks volumes about the complexity of relationships in just a few minutes. It brings the subtext of the situation to the fore in much the same way as Woody Allen does in *Annie Hall* (see Chapter 5) and is an innovative use not only of the short form but of the role sound plays in storytelling, discussed further in Chapter 12.

Finally, *How to Tell When a Relationship is Over* offers both an episodic and cyclical narrative that consists of one situation repeated over and over again. The central premise sees a couple breaking up in vitriolic circumstances, and each scene offers the same event (breaking up) with the same characters in the same location (their kitchen). In one way it is more of a comedic sketch than a narrative, but repeated viewings bear out an underlying deeper structure that offers progression, rising action and resolution, albeit in an unconventional way. There is no plot beyond the central event (breaking up) but the many ways it is presented creates pace, rhythm and forward momentum. The severity of the behaviour the couple displays towards each other gradually increases over the ten minutes, creating rising action and playing with narrative expectation. As the audience watches the same event repeated, they become familiarised with the characters and bring their own expectations and sympathies to the narrative, which are subverted and offered back as genre satire. By the end, although they have talked of the break up many times, it finally happens (the woman is no longer there), giving a sense of pathos and emotional resolution. In this masterpiece of comic timing, narrative is offered in terms of rhythm and deep structure rather than plot or character progression (as discussed in Chapter 10), and still works as an effective story in its own right, not just a series of collated events. From these examples, it can be seen that the short can encompass a variety of narrative approaches and structures, to challenge, inspire and experiment, either to function in its own right or to feed back fresh innovative ideas into more mainstream forms.

Character and psychology

Understanding people and the unconscious self (related to mythology) can aid writers in developing characters and deepen stories. Some industry professionals even go as far as advising students to undertake the study of psychology before specialising in writing.[1] As discussed in Chapter 2, screenwriters need to be crucially aware that character and structure are strongly connected and, for the most part, it is character that dictates story. Screenwriting as an art form enigmatically pulls audiences into itself and relies upon their emotional participation to generate success. William Indick proposes that:

> Audiences are not consciously aware of the subtle manipulation achieved through a film's activation of their primal fears, childhood anxieties, unconscious issues, and repressed desires. Yet, they experience heightened states of arousal when viewing the film, because they are emotionally and psychologically integrated with the characters and images on the screen.
>
> (2004: xii)

So, if psychology of character can be explored and researched by the screenwriter, it is likely the screenplay will take a forward leap into better crafted, more resonant expression.

Both William Indick and Christopher Vogler are contemporary screenwriting authors who use the work of Carl Jung to demonstrate how psychology is inherent in screen characters and the journeys they take. They outline Jung's *archetypes of character*, a set of universal character types Jung saw as working on an unconscious level and manifesting themselves through everyday culture. For Indick, '[w]hereas the archetypes have been depicted for thousands of years through mythology, religion, legends, stories, and art – the primary instrument for the expression of contemporary archetypes is the modern mass medium of movies' (Ibid.: xiv); for Vogler, 'archetypes are part of the universal language of storytelling, and a command of their energy is as essential to the writer as breathing ... Storytellers instinctively choose characters and relationships that resonate to the energy of the archetypes, to create dramatic experiences that are recognisable to everyone' (1999: 22–30). For the working screenwriter, Jung's archetypes can have a twofold function: first, they enable a writer to see them in action when analysing existing drama and glean how they operate; second, the writer can use this knowledge in character and story creation, assessing the function and status of characters according to how they may be approached psychologically.

Perhaps the most useful Jungian archetype for screenwriters is that of *the hero*. This term has been adopted widely in screenwriting to account for the protagonist, and refers strongly to Joseph Campbell's work *The Hero with a Thousand Faces*.[2] In short, this is the archetype that represents the self; and because the self can appear in many forms, it can be a hero with a thousand faces. No matter what the physicality, personality or sociology of a hero character, in archetypal form he or she 'represents the ego's search of wholeness and identity' (Vogler, 1999: 35). The hero is a manifestation of the personal, undertaking a quest where 'internal guardians, monsters, and helpers' (Ibid.) are confronted and integrated to enable completion. When considering the many guises a hero archetype can take, it is useful to bear in mind Indick's notion of *persona*. The hero wears a mask in the story world (2004: 115), meaning he or she is physically individual and unique; what lies beneath is the universal archetype. This relates to notions of physicality and emotionality: on the outside heroes express their identity through wearing a mask (appearance, role, environment, voice) yet on the inside, their emotional resonance speaks volumes to the audience who can connect with shared feelings. The *shadow* is another important archetype for screenwriters as it represents the antagonist. Alongside the hero, the shadow represents the psychology of opposites. Jung believed in Eastern philosophies which pronounce the need for opposing forces in order to create natural balances. In screenwriting terms, the natural balance is the complete, resolved screenplay; it can thus only be achieved by a series of forces opposing the hero's journey. Indick notes that the shadow is 'the repressed alter ego, the dim reflection of our unconscious selves' (Ibid.: 116). This means we can view the antagonist as a reflection of the hidden, dark side of the protagonist. When the protagonist is forced to face the antagonist, it is actually themselves who they are facing. Dramatically, the villainous character forces the hero to take action because the hero does not want to fall into the darker side of their personality. As Vogler states: 'When the protagonist is crippled by doubts or guilt, acts in self-destructive ways, expresses a death wish, gets carried away with his success, abuses his power, or becomes selfish rather than self-sacrificing, the Shadow has overtaken him' (1999: 72).

An understanding of how the antagonist can be seen to represent the darker parts of the protagonist is highly useful for the screenwriter. Through the careful creation of character in early stages of development (see Chapter 2), the writer can ascertain what it is that drives the protagonist to succeed in their goal. This information, such as an understanding of their greatest fear, can then manifest into the antagonist. This will almost certainly raise the stakes for the protagonist who will ardently battle against opposing forces in order not to be defeated.

Many more Jungian archetypes are discussed by writers like Indick and Vogler, and can work extremely well in exploring meaning of characters and suggest ways they can function in the narrative. Similar to classic character functions outlined in Vladimir Propp's *Morphology of the Folktale*, Vogler describes the psychological and dramatic functions of the *mentor* (wise old man or woman), *threshold guardian, herald, shape-shifter* and the *trickster* (1999: 35–75), giving useful examples for clear illustration. Indick follows up his take on Jung with a description of Rollo May's *Archetypes for the Age of Narcissism* (2004: 219–29). These character types result from a theory of narcissism found in (particularly) American culture, fuelled by individualism, independence and isolationism. May's categorisation includes the *cowboy hero, lone crusader, mad scientist* and the *isolated genius*, all types 'that are engrained in the American hero depicted in Hollywood films' (Ibid.: 219). For the screenwriter, this work is invaluable because it goes some way in exploring and explaining why (mainstream) films are fascinated with certain characters, which can be analysed and incorporated into work.

Reflections on character and psychology thus highlight the importance for screenwriters to dedicate themselves to research outside of the immediate realm of screenwriting, whether it may be critical texts on the role of archetypes or narrative function, or reading around subjects such as psychology, anthropology, history or mythology. Rather than seeing such 'distant' research as a chore, it should be considered with pleasure. The writer's journey is one of constantly developing an understanding of characters and the worlds in which they operate. Psychological insights, whether specific to a character or more general as a concept, will no doubt further the writing of the screenplay and the learning of the writer. Stretching the mind now will fertilise the task to come.

Writing the real

In any televisual or filmic form, character is of the essence. Strong, engaging characters who undertake interesting and resonant journeys are the staple not only of drama, but also documentary and reality programming. People become subjects; yet, they too are characters. As Murray Smith argues, '[e]ven if we acknowledge the massive determining power of material and ideological structures, our immediate experience of the social world is through agency – agents filling the roles assigned to them by these structures' (1995: 18). Thus, whereas structure may be pertinent in documentary and reality programming to tell the story, it is through character that an audience experiences the journey and understands the meaning. An exploration of 'real people' stories is useful for the speculative screenwriter because it fosters further notions of how character and plot are linked, and how when people or events in question are factual, creative license comes into play.

  With the explosion of reality TV and factual programming since the late 1990s, there has been an increased fascination with real life people and real life stories. From *Driving School* to *Supernanny*, *Big Brother* to *Little Angels*, international TV has proliferated in giving viewers a slice of their nation's varied lives. Getting children ready for school and arguing about who cooks the dinner are events no longer confined to the privacy of personal domestic life; they are there, in widescreen, for all to view, criticise and compare themselves with. As Friedman argues, reality-based programming does not simply represent a shift in television tastes but 'the industry's reliance on 'reality' as a promotional marketing tool' (2002: 7). A way of dramatists appropriating the successes of reality TV is through the production of stories about real events and real people. Television of late has seen a steady increase in such dramas, and film has maintained a healthy interest in 'living ever close to the real world' of sports and movie stars, musicians, politicians and criminals. Derek Paget (1998; 2004) has conducted much research on the subject and notes quite rightly that the form of factual drama comes in many guises, each one offering a slightly different sense of focus.[3] For the purpose of this discussion, we would like to share the view of Richard Kilborn (1994: 61–2) and refer to this form of story-telling as *documentary drama*. This differs from *drama documentary*, which as Kilborn suggests is primarily a documentary but with elements of added drama to reconstruct certain aspects of the story. *Documentary drama*, rather, is derived from real events but portrays itself in a much more blatant dramatic (fictional) style. We offer its definition as this: a film or television production which mixes the conventions of drama and documentary with the aim of telling a real story, but the use of drama as its central form indicates that the story will be in some way altered to adhere to pre-determined narrative expectations.

The following is a critical insight into the production and reception of documentary drama, assessing how dramatisation processes work for industry and audience and how this links into speculative ideas surrounding subjects and ideas. More importantly, we will offer a structural framework to use in two ways: by writers of documentary drama to evaluate factual material and organise it into a functioning dramatic structure; and by critics who want to understand the way documentary drama works to achieve its desired outcome of telling a story.

Story and plot

Linda Seger notes that fictionalisation is 'a process that demands rethinking, reconceptualizing, and understanding how the nature of drama is intrinsically different from the nature of all other literature' (1992: 2), so when translated to documentary drama (fictionalisation) is an indication of the necessity to consider what the heart of the story is going to be. Rather than simply relaying events in a chronological order from an objective point of view (so-called traditional documentary), documentary drama differs because it needs a more subjective central purpose to drive the drama. Usually the story of a documentary drama brings a particular slant of the history, event or person being explored; the uncovering of a new truth, told from a different point of view. These 'ways in' act as the underpinning story to the narrative in question. It can be argued that writers and producers carefully use the tools of drama to achieve a specific desired (audience) outcome, which may be a political bias, personal affiliation or an attempt to re-write

history. This begs ethical questions around truth which are important
when considering screen ideas critically: Whose story is this? Who is
funding the production? What does that company stand to gain from
the release? Does the drama coincide with current political agendas?
Is this truth, representation, or myth?

As discussed previously, there are clear distinctions between the
notions of *story* and *plot*. Where story exists as a universal, mythical
and somewhat ideological statement, plot is the means of telling it in
a dramatic fashion. When evaluating the process of fictionalisation in
the documentary drama, writers are privileged in that the plot (series
of events) already exists; the facts of events, people and places provide a reasonably strong idea of the basic plot line. What needs to be
found within this plot is the story. The writer has to consider how to use
a plot that already exists to tell a drama driven by thematic subtext.
To reiterate Robert McKee, the 'archetypal story unearths a universally
human experience, then wraps itself inside a unique, culture-specific
expression' (1999: 4). In other words, all stories at heart share common
themes; what defines them is the way they are told; the plot. In documentary drama, the 'unique expression' is already in place because
events and characters are there; they happened. What needs to be constructed is the 'universally human experience', the heart of the story.
If we accept this process of 'finding' a story within an already established plot, essentially a fabricated and contrived process, it stands
to reason the documentary drama could be viewed cautiously. Paget
writes that it 'uses the sequence of events from a real historical occur-
rence or situation and the identities of the protagonists to underpin a
film [or television] script intended to provoke debate about the significance of the events/occurrence' (1998: 82). What strikes us about this
quotation is the use of the word 'underpin.' Rather than stating that
this type of dramatic production is *about* the subject, Paget suggests
the heart of the story lies elsewhere, and that the people, places and
general facts are merely a way of bringing this underlying idea to the
fore. Moreover, Paget's view that the real-life situation is used to 'provoke
debate' is another marker that the subject matter is somewhat vulnerable and can be manipulated to achieve the needs of the writer. In this
way the dramatic/fictional element of telling a real-life story can be
understood as filling an *information gap*. To use Keith Beattie's analysis
of the form, the drama surrounding fact 'provides a way of invoking
psychological or emotional motivations capable of rendering human
actions intelligible' (2004: 153). This is clearly suggestive of a desired story
manipulation, seeking that the audience understands and hopefully

accepts the 'truth' being told. In broad but useful terms, documentary drama differs from documentary in that rather than telling us *what* happened and *how*, it aims to tell us *why*.

If narrative pleasure is a key feature of mainstream film and television, then writers of documentary drama must adhere to screenwriting models to make their work pleasurable and sellable. These models can also be used as a framework to recreate plot from given events and tease out the desired story. In this way structure can be seen as working on two levels: it is a *solution* to help mould the story, yet at the same time creates a *problem* of truth and commitment to reality. If structures of historical or personal events are subject to change, this suggests the screenplay has potential to purvey a new truth. By offering a framework to analyse ways in which true-life stories are presented, we are not proposing a model to radically affect how such stories are made or viewed; rather, one which can be applied to existing models to give writers and critics the tools to evaluate ways in which factual stories have been structured dramatically. In this model we explore *framing*, *focus*, *selection* and *resolution* decoding ways in which the screenplay has been encoded to bring about a desired story outcome.

Framing

Framing is how the screenplay physically begins. For the writer, consideration of how the audience can be posited into a desired location which suggests from the very outset *this* is the story that is going to be told. From a writer's point of view, this could involve positioning the audience so they will accept a preconceived decision to follow a particular angle of the story. Backstory is nearly always portrayed in the opening minutes of drama, and can be a vital tool to frame the protagonist, such as giving the audience, via pre-story events, insights into the life which relates to the central story. Openings can also be framed with the use of voiceover as Paget comments:

> [Voiceover] function is threefold: to start us off with the necessary prior knowledge of the non-story world; to help the story take temporal and locational leaps as the narrative unfolds; and to project us back into the real (non-story) world at the end of the film.
>
> (2004: 198–9)

We would go one step further and suggest voiceover can be primarily used to create instant identification with the protagonist in order to become the audience's *hero*, suggesting their point of view will be the one offered and that any emotion stirred up will be intrinsically linked to their journey within the narrative. Rhetorically, this can be judged as an effective tool for writers to supply an audience with the desired intention; for scholars, it raises questions about truth and morality, there being a danger that the framing will be susceptible to passive audiences to take it as absolute truth.

Focus

The moments directly following the opening are assigned the role of focus: the way in which the drama is geared towards the main agenda. The first actions taking place after the opening serve to clarify that the audience is aware whose story this is and why they are following it. Having established the protagonist, what is their dramatic problem? Why should the audience care about this character? What makes them want the protagonist to succeed? In essence, what is this story really going to tell us? What is the focus? Seger tells us that in biopic movies, 'people's whole lives cannot simply be presented to us. Film's insistence on structure demands that a certain angle or take on the subject has to be articulated to audiences' (1992: 49–50). Ideological as this may be, suggesting the need for dramatic qualities over simple facts, it poses questions for writers which go some way to test their ideas and marketability. At which point does the audience join this character's story? Finding the right moment to start the narrative journey can have significant impact upon how the story is received. Continued identification with the protagonist is also important, and once a writer knows what they want to do with a true-life story, the script can quickly focus towards inducing that agenda.

Selection (Persuasion)

In crude terms, the writer's job is to persuade an audience that what he or she says is true, or at least valid. In this way, careful selection of the events to be told – and those left out – will determine how the story is 'accepted' by the audience. Just like marketing and advertising, rhetoric and persuasion are used to evoke from the audience the desired emotional outcome. Moreover, the use of screenwriting tools can be used to manipulate and persuade the audience into reading a situation differently than they may have previously. For example, the writer may choose to show the protagonist in dangerous situations where they are seen as vulnerable. This may result in a sympathetic reaction from the audience, which would raise interesting questions if the protagonist presented were an internationally infamous criminal. Furthermore, and as noted by Paget (2004: 203), writers may develop or even invent characters to impart upon the narrative a rhetorical slant. Taking the above scenario, a newly invented character could be added to the story world to act as an antagonistic force against the protagonist, resulting in a subsequent view of the criminal as victim. This can clearly be seen as an act of selection and appropriation to create persuasion. It is the essence of selection (persuasion); the use of structure and dramatic technique to invoke a reaction within the audience that matches the intended. This again raises questions around authenticity and ideology, but in screenwriting is there ever space to tell a story from an objective point of view? Can a writer ever tell a story *as it is* if there has to be a central premise or controlling idea?

Resolution

The resolving of the documentary drama can be seen as the key factor in determining what the story is about and how the audience should feel. It is the stage of the screenplay where all events come to a climax, and final sense is made of the character journey. Looking critically, it could be deemed crucial for the writer to consider how the ending will crystallise and make clear the intention, angle and focus of the story. As the audience walks out of the cinema or exits the living room, the resolution can leave them with a deep-felt sense of dramatic closure and catharsis, which in documentary drama will often have a statement attached. Audiences are at their own liberty to accept, reject or negotiate rhetorical signs, but for a writer, direction and focus has to be clear. An open, ambiguous ending may provide a dissatisfactory feeling among the audience who, inevitably, are seeking closure (whether they agree with the statement being made or not.) Various techniques of writing resolutions may be used to punctuate the story and persuade the audience: there may be a montage of images to reflect upon the core argument; a recap of the main themes and evidence pointing towards the intended outcome. The use of voiceover could be reintroduced to pose final opinions and, if the narrator is the subject, to act as a final attempt at creating identification and empathy. Some documentary dramas favour the use of a title card containing information about what 'really happened.' This may be a way of shocking the audience who so far may have been so absorbed in the story world that they have forgotten the real events. If trying to justify someone's actions, then this technique may indeed stir up questions in the audience about whether or not the subjects deserve what they got. However the writer chooses to resolve the screenplay, it is clear that something with impact is required to imply, if not persuade, what the final feelings should be. The techniques used reinforce how the codes embedded within the narrative should be decoded by the audience.

What this framework offers is an insight into how specifically real life stories are worked upon in order to create structurally successful documentary dramas. If the whole purpose of writing a screenplay is to try and relay a message, then the notions of framing, focus, selection (persuasion) and resolution certainly seem to operate when looking at true-life fictionalisation.

A brief but useful example of this framework is *Monster*. Following the life of America's so-called first female serial killer Aileen Wuornos, this film offers the audience an insight into the convicted murderer as a victim. Rather than condemning her actions and portraying her negatively, it seeks to uncover some of the reasons why Wuornos killed. Framing is constructed with this victim view in mind. A voiceover of Wuornos details how, as a child, she wanted to be just like every other girl. She wanted to look glamorous; be wanted; be loved. This is juxtaposed with visual images depicting her actual childhood: she is abused, loses her innocence, is cast-off by men who see her purely as a sexual object. The combination (contradiction) of images and sound portray Wuornos as a victim of both her childhood and society, suggesting reasons why she may have turned out the way she did. Following this opening sequence *Monster* quickly focuses and selects scenes which depict Wuornos as a hopeless individual whose only hope is to hold onto any love she can find; in this case that of her newly found girlfriend. It is this desire for love, to be loved, to rid herself of past and present abuse from men that drive the film. Far from the hardened, sick and vile creature which audiences may have pre-conceived, Aileen Wuornos is portrayed in a sympathetic light. The audience is given reasons to understand why, perhaps, she did what she did. She is seen being raped by a man who picks her up, triggering memories of her childhood. It is implied that she sees these men as versions of her father (and others) who abused her as a child. The film uses material like this to suggest she is seeking revenge for the psychological damage she has been left with, portraying her as a victim and raising questions about whether or not she was the hardened serial killer she was branded as. The film's resolution depicts the moment where she was tricked by her girlfriend into admitting her crimes. This becomes very pertinent for the audience who can see that the only person she has ever truly loved or who has loved her has turned her back on her. This seems to be the central driving force of the narrative; a story about betrayal and losing faith in the people who are supposed to look after you. As Wuornos is given the execution order, emotions rise in the final minutes of the film. She yells 'sending a raped woman to execution!' in the courtroom which, assuming the audience has followed the intended line of sympathy, evokes a deep sense of pity. Linking back to the start, her voiceover is again used to depict her loss of hope in humanity. Her words, criticising the use of anecdotes which try and make people feel that things will always turn out good in the end, ring darkly for the audience. This is her view of life because it is the life she has led; she is a sad victim.

10   Structures and Narratives

The purpose of this chapter is to explore how narrative structure can be challenged, rejecting traditionalist mainstream ideas, and at the same time offer critical reinforcements about what purpose structure serves. Some of the alternative structures suggested, breaking away from three acts, are a marker of the times. They offer ways in which screenwriters can experiment with storytelling chronology, challenging audience perceptions of and interactions with narrative. Flashbacks, multiple protagonists, parallel and sequential narratives are all ways of breaking the mainstream mould; yet, crucially, they still need to work for an audience. Narrative pleasure and story coherence are still rudimentary components of screenwriting, and sometimes those who challenge the rules are in fact doing little more than reshaping them. The chapter will also revisit notions of story and dramatic pleasure, discussing how narrative structure embodies ideology and serves societal intent.

The purpose of structure

One recent problem with discussions around structure is that it is seen as an easy template to compare scripts to and help producers or executives see if it hits the 'right' notes. But thinking about structure should not be a corrective straitjacket strategy. What is amiss with many current formal and informal debates concerning structure is that its purpose is not understood fully. Writers, developers and producers often confuse 'understanding structure' with 'understanding three act structure', but they are not one and the same. Three act structure is a type of structure; structure in general is a tool to understanding and shaping story, with two main functions:

(1)   It provides a way of *ordering information*, to reveal story facts and events to the audience in the most appropriate sequence, making it intelligible and engaging in a way suitable to the genre and tone.

(2) It creates a *pattern of emotion* in both character and audience through rhythm, pace and tone, crucial in establishing a deeper connection between audience and story.

Structure as character arc and theme

Beyond pragmatic reasons, there are poetic and emotional reasons why structure is crucial to good screenwriting. A well-formed structure relates closely to character and emotion, and instead of restricting character, structure (as in character arcs) is a way to crack them open and tease out deeper answers to who they really are. In a similar way, structure is connected to theme. A well-written story goes beyond structure as not simply a way of ordering information or keeping the audience engaged, but engages 'deep structure' to mirror and enhance theme. As discussed in Chapter 3, there are two levels of narrative structure: order of events (plot) and emotional character arc (story). In a surprisingly large number of seemingly non-linear plots (order of events told in a non-chronological manner), the underlying emotional character arc progresses forward in a linear fashion. The character grows emotionally as they undertake their journey, whether it is caused by linearly arranged events or not. This is the case with both *Memento* and *Groundhog Day* (see case studies below), and it is this emotional progression that makes an otherwise potentially art-house or experimental story break out and attract wider appeal; it offers an emotionally familiar character journey at its core. Truly non-linear screen stories that do not have this at their heart are much rarer, and rarely commercially successful since they do not offer character arc satisfaction.

Structure as music

An even deeper purpose to structure is to create an emotional reaction and response in the audience. Parallels exist between screenwriting and film editing since they are both concerned with ordering information and making a story intelligible, while creating rhythm and pace that moves the audience from one moment to the next in a way relevant to the emotion, mood or genre. But working with structure is also akin to working with music, where the structuring of story emotion is not dissimilar to the way a composer orchestrates emotion through the flow of a song. In screenwriting, meaning is created through *form*

as well as *content*, and the pace and flow of a screenplay shapes the
viewing experience. The audience may not be aware of it, but structure is
a powerful emotional tool; by placing one scene next to another (working with transitions), a writer creates meaning between scenes through
their comparing or contrasting relationship; and by shortening or
elongating moments, the writer creates subconscious almost physical reactions in the audience as they hold their breath, feel their hearts
pumping, cry, laugh and fear. These emotions are created as much by
the form of the overall *pattern and order* (structure) as they are by the
content of a moment (scene). One cannot exist without the other; a
scene is quickly forgotten if it does not fit into the whole in a satisfying
or relevant way.

The way a story is structured thus has both intellectual meaning
and direct emotional impact. It provides a form and a pattern for the
content, and depending on its shape, the content necessarily changes.
In this way structure becomes part of the landscape of a story, not solely
about rules and restrictions but about expressing character journey,
theme and emotion as much as dialogue or visual metaphor. Structure
is about the subconscious, the subtle, the sublime. When a writer has
truly considered the form as well as the content of a story and chosen the most relevant and resonant structure to unfold it in, structure
becomes a potent tool which should be rejoiced in. We would thus like
to reposition structure as an emotional rather than technical tool. Structure should not be decided upon away from the story; it is an essential
part of the story and should grow from within. Structure is about building and constructing narrative, whatever pattern the writer chooses;
orchestrating and unfolding the emotion of character and audience;
and finding the best way to express and shape that journey.

Linear emotion in non-linear plot

Groundhog Day tells the story of Phil, mysteriously stuck in the same
day over and over until he learns the lesson of unselfish love. The story
structure is about repetition, and although the surface plot seems
non-linear (cyclical), the underlying *emotional* structure progresses in
a broadly linear fashion through Phil's reactions to his (unchanging)
surroundings. It is a truly character-driven story since only by the protagonist's change can the story find meaning. Acts and sequences in
Groundhog Day are created by internal emotional change, not external
physical development. At first Phil reacts to his situation in shock and

disbelief; unable to believe what has happened he tests the world to see if it is really true (this also helps establish the world by creating credibility and internal logic). The first act ends when Phil realises, after getting drunk in a bar and almost dying by driving along a train track, that if nothing ever changes, he can do whatever he wants without consequence. This ushers in a whole new sequence where Phil begins to enjoy his world and exploit it in the most self-indulgent way possible – nothing has changed except for Phil's view of it. After this, the structure is divided up according to the character's progression in relation to who he is in the world: at first he is happy and carefree, but as he spends more time with Rita he falls in love. He tries to woo her but realises she is not going to be as easy as Nancy. Phil thus has a new goal: to find out everything he can about Rita in order to create her perfect date. Eventually he manages this with remarkable success, until the final crushing moment when Rita insists she will never go to bed with him on a first date. Thus, whatever Phil does, he will never win Rita because he only has endless first dates.

This midpoint crisis plunges him into depression, trying first to kill the groundhog then himself. Nothing works so he finally moves to honesty, telling Rita he thinks he is immortal and asking for her help (he has become vulnerable). She agrees to spend the day with him and they have another 'perfect date', but this time an honest, rather than manipulative one. At the end of Act 2, the audience truly believes Phil loves her (as opposed to the chat-up line he used at the midpoint); however, Rita is asleep and does not hear his declaration. In Act 3, Phil has moved into acceptance. He spends his endless one day helping others and improving himself. He becomes unselfish and transforms into a man we know Rita would want, but he only gets Rita by giving her up. He no longer actively pursues her, instead spending his day being a good citizen and enjoying the small things in life. In the climax sequence the dynamic of their relationship is reversed, Rita bidding for him at the bachelor auction (she wants him as opposed to him pursuing her). Phil has become a better, wiser, selfless man and as they spend the night together, he is finally able to tell her he loves her – and this breaks the spell. The structure of *Groundhog Day* can thus be seen to be both linear (in character progression) and cyclical (in ordering of events), and it is in this combination that the theme is so richly expressed.

Much has been discussed about *Memento* and it sometimes seems to be deemed a postmodernist 'champion', employed to prove the timely demise of three act structure. Like Tarantino a decade before, it has inspired a generation of novice writers who churn out copycats and swear by new 'anti-rules'. However, a closer analysis of this film's structure shows that just like *Groundhog Day*, *Memento*'s emotional structure is clearly linear. Contrary to popular opinion, this film does not simply have a backwards structure but actually utilises two structures: a backwards movement interwoven with a static flashback. The static flashback is shot in black and white with voiceover, whereas the backwards movement is in colour and more naturalistic. There are two reasons for the inclusion of the static flashback, one pragmatic and one thematic. Narrating a backwards movement creates obvious difficulties with transitions since scenes do not actually play backwards but forwards; it is simply the order in which the scenes are shown that has been reversed. The structure could thus become jerky when segments are linked together, so the static flashback serves as a device to smooth over the joins and allow for a slight breather before jumping backwards once more. It also allows for clear exposition which makes sense of the potentially confusing backward segments, while interweaving the story of Sammy, which at first seems a throwaway story within a story, but is later revealed as essential to the protagonist's life and mission. The static flashback also works thematically since Leonard is stuck and unable to move forward. He has lost his short-term memory and constantly has to reassemble the pieces of his life to seek their meaning (just as the structure asks the audience to do). He can remember his past, indeed feels this is the only time he knows who he is, but as he continually attempts to piece together information, the static flashback reveals the moment (almost floating out of time) that is at its core. The dual devices of moving *backwards* and staying in a *static* flashback are highly appropriate for a story about a man obsessed with investigating a *past* mystery ('Who killed my wife?') but is in reality *stuck* in emotional trauma, unable to move forward. Indeed, at the end of the film it is revealed that both strategies are false since the 'murderer' of his wife has already been 'caught': both when Teddy helped him to find the man responsible for the initial attack; and by forcing Leonard to come to terms with the fact that there was no Sammy, that Sammy's story happened to Leonard and that he, not Sammy, killed his own wife by injecting her (unknowingly) with too much insulin. In this way, the structure creates an emotional pattern of confusion, disorientation and entrapment in one continual moment for both character and audience. It bears out the theme of a man unable to move on after bereavement, only able to look backwards while fooling himself he is moving forwards, becoming pathologically locked into his grief.

So, how can such a complicated and potentially confusing structure tell such an engaging story? The answer lies in the use of a structure which actually moves the audience forward. First of all, this is essentially a mystery story and though the sequence of events may be unravelling backwards, the *audience's knowledge* of that mystery (finding out information, putting clues together) is deepening and moving forwards. Engagement is also created through the linearity of the character arc where, although plot is moving backwards, for the audience, the character is unfolding and progressing forwards. Leonard is finding out more about himself (as is the audience), though he constantly worries about not knowing who he is. He also finds out more about the mystery as he journeys through the story, feeling he is getting closer to solving it. The tattoos on his body by which he orientates himself are the concrete visual representation of this building of knowledge: he keeps gathering the clues, building his case, adding information to his skin. By the end, Teddy challenges Leonard that he has already achieved what he set out to do but cannot remember it, and is now involved in 'creating a puzzle you can never solve'. This is what the structure can also be seen to do: offering a constant puzzle in every new segment, though at the end giving the audience the satisfaction of a resolution that answers most of their questions. In a way the whole story of the film is a sham, as the 'real' plot (taking revenge on John G) has already happened before the audience joins the film. The audience, just like Leonard, is denied experiencing the real revenge. In this way the structure mirrors and resonates the themes of the film: confined by grief, unable to move on, never satisfied with the revenge already played out. That is the tragedy of Leonard, though unlike him, the story offers a way out for the audience, solving its mystery at the end and providing a resolution.

The flashback narrative

The use of flashback in screenwriting can be dated as far back as the 1940s, with films such as *Citizen Kane* and *Brief Encounter*. In these films the story told in flashback (the past) is integral to the whole, allowing the audience to experience that which has already happened and make connections to the present. Linda Aronson writes that through this type of narrative technique, 'the audience can relive the past rather than just hearing about it … flashback narrative structure uses a series of flashbacks to construct an entire story in the past that runs in tandem with a story in the present' (2001: 107). Flashback highlights a past event and its importance to the present without worry of being expositional. Rather than characters relaying former events and feelings through dialogue, the audience can witness them. Although the flashback is not a new story technique, it is an increasingly popular method of screenwriting which has not only infiltrated television, but one which has found new ways of operating within film: the *flash forward* and *flash out of time*. In flash forward, instead of witnessing how former events have come to influence the present, future events are experienced to show the audience what *may* happen. In other words, if a character is making a decision about what to do in a given situation, the audience may see a flash forward which predicts the future effects of this decision. This may work to clarify the decision and prove it is a good one; alternatively, it may suggest it would be a bad one, portraying some of the possible negative outcomes. In flash out of time either the future is portrayed or, in many cases, an alternative to the present reality. Flash out of time is usually a quick glimpse of another version of the situation a character is in, often used for comic effect. If a character is bored of a conversation, for example, a flash out of time may work like a daydream and present what the character wishes she were doing instead. This technique is common in television shows like *Hollyoaks* and *Scrubs*. In both cases, the flash out of time is used for stylistic effect aimed at the audience demographic (young, trendy, used to visual style experimentation) but is also of narrative importance since it offers a comedic alternative reality to the present. In *Scrubs*, J.D. often daydreams about his colleagues and momentarily sees them in a different light to how they really are; then flashes back to reality and re-joins the scene, often somewhat begrudgingly. In *Hollyoaks*, light-hearted scenes see characters thinking 'out of time', envisaging scenarios of what would happen if...

Types of flashback

The most common type of flashback narrative is the *book-ended*. This is where the majority of the story is located within the past, the flashback story surrounded by a present story: the drama starts in the present, then flashes back, then returns to the present for final resolution. Films which use this technique include *The Green Mile*, *Titanic* and *The Bridges of Madison County*. In these, an inciting incident in the present leads to the need for the past to be told in order to resolve the challenge the inciting incident has set. *The Bridges of Madison County*, for example, begins where the recently deceased Francesca's diary is found by her children clearing the house. The story then told in the past explains the contents of the diary and why it was written, how Francesca sacrificed her own happiness for the sake of her children. The flashback story has its own three act structure and is then inserted into a bigger narrative, incorporating the three acts and extending them to serve an overall narrative problem, conflict and resolution. The book-ended parts may only be short, but are crucial since they give the raison d'être for the flashback. Without the present, with its inciting incident and resolution, the flashback stories float aimlessly. Nevertheless, as Aronson concurs, the story in the past is more important than the story in the present (Ibid.: 108). What we highlight here is that *the past drives the overall narrative*. The flashback is the emotional journey which explains or relieves the problem a character faces in their present physical journey. Of course the past story has its own physical journey as well, but the essence of it is to provide the emotional understanding of the physical problem experienced in the present.

Aronson outlines two other uses of flashback narrative important to a fuller understanding of the possibilities of the technique. The first is *flashback as illustration*. Often accompanied by voiceover, this is depicted on screen in fragments rather than as a continuous story, detailing what has happened or, in the case of flash forward, what could/will happen (Ibid.). This technique is often used in detective or crime stories, whereby the audience finally realises who the murderer was and crime committed. In these dramas the flashback as illustration may appear as distorted, incomplete fragments throughout the narrative, which Aronson calls *flashback as life-changing incident*. This is where 'one ominous, incomplete flashback occurs incrementally throughout the film until, at the film's climax, it appears in its shocking entirety, revealing the mysteries and motives of the protagonist' (Ibid.). In the detective or crime drama this can serve to tease an audience hungry for the truth, and will eventually be played out in full when the details of the crime are revealed. A story which employs this technique skilfully is Kate O'Riordan's UK TV drama *The Return*. The story's protagonist Lizzie Hunt (Julie Walters) is subjected to a series of intermittent flashbacks about what actually happened on the night her husband was killed. She (and the audience) are led to believe she murdered him in a drunken stupor, but after her release she tries in vain to access the real truth. The flashbacks occur only partially as Lizzie struggles along her journey, but each time more information is slowly released. They act to haunt her, to challenge her thoughts, and involve the audience in cracking the mystery. At the drama's climax, where she confronts her father about his involvement, the fragments cease to be incomplete and the haunting life-changing incident is revealed. The audience witnesses the past events, finally understanding the whole story and learning the truth. As with any flashback narrative, moments from the past are integrated into the present to resolve the character's dramatic problem.

Multiple protagonist narratives

Growing away from traditional 'single hero' narratives, which follow the plight of one character with one set of dramatic problems, some narratives follow the journey of more than one hero. This enables the audience to experience the growth of a multitude of characters with varying dramatic problems, and if experienced alongside one another in the same story, invites the audience to make links between characters and gain insights into how one situation or theme can generate a range of responses. Both *multiple protagonist* and *parallel story* narratives allow for this experience, enabling the audience to journey through an intertwined narrative with a set of main characters. The multiple protagonist narrative can be defined as dramas which feature more than one protagonist living in the same story world, and who are brought together by and react to the same inciting incident. Usually in multiple protagonist stories the same physical journey is shared, especially as characters are brought together by the same inciting incident. How the individuals react on a scene-by-scene level is personal, taking into account their emotional drive as a reaction to the inciting incident, but generally speaking they share the same plotline. What an audience experiences in the multiple protagonist narrative is a development of individual emotional journeys where characters learn about themselves from the experience of the same physical environment, reacting not only to the shared action of the journey but also to the experience of being with the other character(s) in the situation.

Before You Go is a multiple protagonist film which explores how the death of a mother brings three sisters together who then go about rediscovering themselves. The inciting incident is the death of Violet Heaney, a catalytic event which forces the three daughters Teresa, Mary and Catherine back to their native Ireland and childhood home. The narrative takes place over less than a week, during which time the daughters prepare Violet's funeral and relive old memories. A crucial theme within the story is that of conflicting memories of the past, each daughter remembering events in a different way and with different outcomes. As the three struggle to make a clear picture of their family past and secrets being unearthed, they also struggle to cope with and tolerate each other. They collide with each other and provide conflict; they are each other's antagonist, but ones necessary for emotional growth. This is an important aspect of the multiple protagonist narrative because each has to work with the others and appropriate their behaviour and feelings accordingly. Caught in a pressurised situation, it forces them to review their relationships and find ways to connect. The individual backstories and problems are explored in a shared story world: Teresa grows from an anal, obsessive, neurotic organiser to open up her heart, reveal her true feelings, and cry for her mother's death. Catherine is an in-your-face, pot-smoking hypochondriac who clings onto the idea of love and happiness with any man who will look at her. Catherine's journey enables her to realise this emotional instability and be honest with herself about her deep loneliness and sadness. Mary is the more successful of the sisters, a doctor. Her journey reveals that at fourteen she had a baby who was secretly adopted. She has held hope ever since that one day he will come to find her, but learns the devastating news that he was killed when he was thirteen. She thus learns to let go of the past and sever her current ties with a married colleague who cannot give her the commitment she needs. Finally, *Before You Go* reinforces the shared inciting incident feature of multiple protagonist narratives by Violet Heaney appearing on several occasions as a ghost. She acts as a constant reminder of the physical binding around which the three daughters have come together. For the audience, she symbolises the need for each character to use the physical situation to overcome their emotional problem.

The Banger Sisters is also in multiple protagonist form, telling the story of long-lost best friends Suzette and Lavinia reunited twenty years on. What is perhaps misleading about this narrative is that the two protagonists do not appear together properly until the end of Act 1; their meet is in fact the act turning point. Prior to this, the audience has followed the story through Suzette's eyes, heading to Phoenix to find Lavinia. Lavinia has appeared briefly, but it is not until her daughter brings her and Suzette together that the multiple protagonist nature of the story truly begins. Some audiences may read the story as a single protagonist film, with Suzette as the hero, but in actual fact when the two meet and the story moves forward both characters share the story load. Lavinia's journey enables her to change from a prim, proper suburban housewife trying to conceal her past as a 'groupie' to allowing herself to 'be free' and show her family who she used to be. Alongside this, the usually sprightly, brash, carefree Suzette comes to realise that she does need love and commitment in her life and envies what Lavinia has achieved with her family and role in the community. Thus, the narrative allows both to change substantially, as much as the other, and because each one relies on the other to change, this is a prime example of the multiple protagonist narrative. Interestingly, the structural element which physically brings Suzette and Lavinia together in the present is Lavinia's daughter. Although she is a product of her mother, a respected student with excellent grades and high school responsibilities, she still likes to take part in the wilder side of life. The film's inciting incident takes place when, at her prom ball, she takes drugs and is left out cold in the hotel corridor. This is where Suzette meets her and helps her, demonstrating hands-on motherly skills which have perhaps been lacking from Lavinia. The next day, Suzette drives her home and meets with Lavinia. Structurally this is a crucial part of the narrative because Lavinia's daughter represents a mixture of the two elders: respected and well educated, but also carefree and a risk taker. Using this character to bring the two protagonists together is a clever way of showing the state both are currently in, and hinting at how spending time together may help them both. It is also a reflection of the past and the two directions in which life can go. *The Banger Sisters* is therefore a story of two protagonists who are confronted with each other in the form of Lavinia's daughter, and forced to admit their failures in later life. Only by taking a journey together can they realise who they are and overcome their internalised problems.

As an ensemble film, *Magnolia* has no single narrative viewpoint. The film opens with a long voiceover that not only introduces the world ('a strange place') and a theme ('are there coincidences?') but also offers the audience a perspective, a way of watching the stories by stepping back, slightly separated yet knowing there will be much to connect them since strange coincidences and events have already been mentioned. Following the opening voiceover and setting, a montage introduces all main characters. Though there are a number, the first act reveals some as more major players than others. It soon becomes clear it is *theme* that connects them: these are lonely people, characters suffering the pain of broken relationships, loss and sadness, either denying or living in the past and now finding it catching up with them, a challenge to rebuild lost relationships and lives. The ensemble structure shows the audience how many lonely people there are in a far more effective way than following a story of one; it is the sheer volume of cases and their similar situations that is the core of this story. What makes the film so successful is not just wonderful acting and poignant scenes, but the way the screenplay moves the audience through the sprawling ensemble and allowing each main character to progress forward emotionally. When each character's strand is separated from the ensemble, it is clear they all more or less follow a mini three act structure, with a crisis and climax in each, moving characters forward emotionally in linear fashion. It offers similar narrative pleasures to more conventionally structured stories in that the audience goes on a journey with the characters, and sees them develop and grow as they are faced with difficult decisions, hard choices and resonant revelations. The overall structure is revealed as meaningful in the way the opening had promised, where connections link the characters together in the most astounding ways. Thus, this *super-structure* reflects the theme of the story by bringing together lonely people and showing them to be connected after all, that there are no coincidences, giving the various strands resonance, drive, cohesion and closure.

City of God is another example of a multiple protagonist narrative. It may almost be deemed a *chaotic narrative*, where characters share the same story environment but are not brought together by an inciting incident. Instead, what truly unites them is the world, where a collection of rambling fast paced lives thread in and out of each other without creating conventionally clear arcs. Its solid narrative anchor comes through the story being as much about a location as the people who inhabit it, both in terms of plot and theme. The world works as a container for all the stories, giving cohesion and focus. It differs from *Magnolia* in that it has a central protagonist (Rocket) through whose eyes most of the story is related, his eventual job as a journalist attempting to document and capture the essence of his *favela*. Though a distinct underlying story strand can be traced, along the way the audience is taken on dizzying tangential rides around the neighbourhood, witnessing personal stories that often take place away from the main character and in flashback. What keeps the audience engaged is partly the sheer energy and pace, but also the strong suspense of never knowing what is going to happen next. The story uses a technique of subverting expectation repeatedly: in flashback one part of the narrative puzzle is shown to make the audience think they know what has happened, only to later reveal there was much more to it and adding another twist, constantly changing the picture that had been defined. It fools the audience into believing they have control over the narrative, only to throw in another point of view to make them question what has been seen. What stops this exponentially increasing story world becoming a nightmarish tangle is the narrative voiceover providing exposition and commentary, drawing separate parts together and clarifying events; anchoring the structure by giving it focus and a point of reference. The structure is a perfect thematic fit as it not only shows the audience the *favela* in a rich, complex and comprehensive way, but in doing so emphasises the chaos, unpredictability and beauty of this world, a place where nothing turns out as expected (by character or audience). This is a constant narrative theme throughout the story and the structure bears it out on a deep level.

It is important not to mistake a multiple protagonist (or ensemble) narrative with a traditional story which simply has other main characters. Although in many films there are subplots and some main or secondary characters experience growth, the multiple protagonist story is specifically about shared protagonists who carry equal dramatic weight and respond to the same inciting incident. An example of this is *American Beauty*, which we feel Linda Aronson wrongly defines as a multiple protagonist narrative (2001). Although Carolyn Burnham does grow and have her own journey, it is nowhere near of the same weight as Lester's nor is it as a reaction to the same inciting incident. Lester is the clear single protagonist, incited to the story by seeing the beautiful, young Angela perform as a cheerleader, and following his drive to attract her attention. Carolyn's journey is more subdued and suggestive from the start of the film as an ongoing battle; not one brought about by a specific story event. Rather, the multiple protagonist story is one where, as in *Magnolia*, characters bear similar weight within the structure and serve either their own arc or the overall theme, rather than the arc of the protagonist. Defining protagonists is ultimately about perspective; whose eyes the audience is invited to experience the narrative through.

Parallel stories

Like multiple protagonist narratives, the parallel (or tandem) story features the journey of more than one hero. It differs in that the protagonists do not necessarily inhabit the same story world, nor do they react to the same inciting incident. Instead, what links the narratives is more conceptual; it could be the type of world the characters inhabit, a theme, a message or motif which runs through the parallel stories.

The narrative is structured so the stories interweave, the audience experiencing each of the protagonists' journeys in parallel fashion, back and forth. *The Hours* is a parallel narrative which explores three stories set in three distinct time frames: 1923, 1951 and 2001. Set in Richmond (England), Los Angeles and New York, they follow the lives of three women connected by the book *Mrs Dalloway*. One of the characters is the book's author Virginia Woolf, the others Laura and Clarissa who in various ways relate to the book in later years. The opening sequence clearly and cleverly formulates the parallel nature of the film, displaying an exhilarating sequence which glides back and forth into each of the characters' lives. The establishing situation is a morning routine, with Virginia, Laura and Clarissa preparing for the day ahead in their respective environments. Character connections and thematic coherence are heightened by the constant intercutting of time frames. Matching shots such as alarms ringing, flowers being displayed and faces being washed create a strong affiliation between the three and provide the audience with a clear indication that the individual stories are part of a larger narrative with thematic connection. As the stories develop and interweave, various themes are embodied in the parallel situations: loneliness, sacrifice, lesbianism and a struggle for voice. Putting them together in three forms within three worlds strengthens the thematic power, as well as creating an interesting relationship between the women and, essentially, Virginia Woolf's book.

The 2007 Channel 4 drama *Clapham Junction* offered a similar audience experience, telling parallel stories of a group of people living in the Clapham area of London. Predominantly focusing on gay men, the drama follows the interactions and conflicts created when people meet with each other in the area. Most of the stories focus upon sexual encounters of some sort, but the real heart to these stories is what the encounters say about society, politics and overall, human emotion. The drama cleverly adopts a structure whereby many of the characters meet each other in various situations, bringing to that character's story their own backstory and agenda, creating a complex set of narratives which collide and melt into each other. The reason that the drama is parallel rather than multiple protagonist is because although the story environment is the same for all characters (Clapham), their worlds are different. Also, each of the protagonists has a different inciting incident to their personal story and the meetings, often chance, are a complex addition to the drama, not ones that confine the characters together as in *Before You Go*.

A crucial element to any parallel story is its interwoven nature. The stories are spliced together to infuse dramatic intrigue into the connectedness of the narratives, and create conflict, variety and pace. Moreover, the interweaving stories work together to clarify a theme or story value, enabling the audience to experience it through a variety of portrayals. Overall, the parallel story can be understood as a collection of interwoven slices of life which combine and build towards the successful composition of one meta-narrative; the theme or controlling idea.

Un film collectif

Premiered at Cannes in 2006, *Paris, Je T'aime* is a collection of eighteen short films by celebrated world directors including Gus Van Sant, Ethan and Joel Coen, Wes Craven, Alexander Payne and Gurinder Chadha. The films vary in style and theme, from real to surreal, logical to fantastical, but are brought together under the umbrella of a celebration of the city. The eighteen films are set in Paris's *arrondissements*, where characters encounter a flash of realisation or a moment of change. These stories encompass a range of themes and human emotions, including love, death, racism, sexuality, grief and loneliness, and are bound by the respective characters' interactions with and movements within the city. Singularly the short films are poignant, but collectively they form a moving and special narrative. Each film has its own mini three act structure, the character encountering an inciting incident, journeying through progressive conflict and change, then reaching a resolution of some sort (not necessarily closure.) Combined, they form a narrative of contemporary Paris where the sequential structure offers the audience powerful insights into life in the city. In some ways this film can be likened to *Sin City*, which again offers the audience a sequential narrative form exploring life in Basin City. Based on Frank Miller's graphic comic series, the film explores some of the stories and characters from the original works but not employing a classically structured format. Like *Paris, Je T'aime*, which uses individual short films rather than individual short comic stories, *Sin City* 'celebrates' (albeit pessimistically) life in the city. The sequential stories have their own internal structure of incitement, conflict and resolution, but the guiding narrative principle of the whole film is the location in which the stories take place. Although *Sin City* does offer some overall resolution, whereby one of the stories is revisited and the city is seen to 'close down,' there is a sense of openness and perhaps not everyone will feel a satisfactory resolution has been reached. *Paris, Je T'aime*, on the other hand, offers a more defined narrative closure. The film ends on the story of an American tourist, Carole, who describes her time holidaying in Paris. She details what the city has to offer and the places she has visited but resolves her narration with a very personal account. Sitting in a park watching passers-by, she recalls how more than anything before in her life, Paris has the ability to make her feel something. Although she has spent most of her life in a lonely existence, she offers that Paris has changed this; here she feels like she is somebody. Her words tell the audience that not only has she fallen in love with Paris, but Paris has fallen in love with her. This clearly points towards a feeling of utter admiration for the city, which almost resolves the overall narrative for the audience by reinforcing what the other stories have in common. In a final sequence, some stories are revisited momentarily where the audience sees the characters in a scene 'post' the film they were in; sometimes the varying characters intertwine with each other. As with the multiple protagonist narrative, this allows the audience to meet the characters once more, remember their stories, and make connections between them to glean a sense of the overall thematic premise.

Closure, pleasure and ideology

As explored throughout this book, narrative pleasure is a crucial feature in mainstream film and television. It is a mechanism by which audiences judge the success of a dramatic text, seeking to find plot points and dramatic junctures which adhere not only to their expectations, but their ability to understand the story told. Even in the alternative structures discussed above, there is a strong sense of narrative coherence. However, closure is a particularly crucial element of a screenplay as it offers a sense of dramatic catharsis with strong audience expectations. Thus we would like to speculate further on narrative pleasure and consider why it forms part of the fabric of a screenplay. To quote Aristotle:

> [Drama] is an imitation of an action that is admirable, complete and possesses magnitude; in language made pleasurable, each of its species separated in different parts; performed by actors, not through narration; effecting through pity and fear the purification of such emotions.
>
> (1996: 10)

This tells us Aristotle believed drama could be defined as having inherent, identifiable components, and that these components can be judged as successful or unsuccessful. Having a story which is *admirable* infers the audience should be involved in a dramatic journey and vying for something substantial like a hero's eventual success or villain's deserved demise, and that a sense of resonance or *magnitude* should be purveyed. These elements tie-in with the idea of being *complete*, alluding to the necessity of narrative pleasure in dramatic structure. This works, arguably, because only when a drama reaches its conclusion, ties up all its story threads and evokes meaning in its audience can it be seen as pleasurable. Aristotle's notion of *purification* is more commonly known as *catharsis*,[1] the moment at which a character ends his or her material journey and gains a physical and/or emotional release. Catharsis can thus be understood as a process of disposing oneself of an excess of emotions in order to reach a greater state of balance. For example, witnessing a character spend much of the drama battling against prolific obstacles and forces requires a moment whereby the character is rewarded for her efforts and troubles. In turn, it is important to note that this manifests itself in the audience too, who feed upon closure and catharsis to obtain a feeling of narrative pleasure and relief.

It is commonly viewed that Aristotle believed plot (or action) is primary, and character (or emotion) secondary: '[w]ell-being and ill-being reside in action, and the goal of life is an activity, not a quality' (1996: 11). Although this suggests Aristotle firmly believed in plot-centred narratives, we believe it has been misinterpreted. Within the quotation there is a clear acknowledgement of a character's emotion: *well-being* and *ill-being* are used to describe someone's state within a given situation, not the situation itself. Therefore, although the belief by many is that Aristotle considered action and plot as the primary constituents of drama, we infer that he was also subconsciously aware of the more internally driven narrative thread of character and emotion.

A speculative question to raise here then is this: does narrative pleasure and catharsis of resolution serve to fulfil an ideological function? If narratives are seen to follow the same patterns, and offer audiences similar emotional experiences, it could be argued these narratives have the ability to generate ideological intention. They are a product of mass culture, and thinkers such as The Frankfurt School would view them cautiously. Rather than offering a wealth of readings or a multitude of possibilities, formulaic narratives which (falsely?) give pleasure to the masses could be seen as limiting, socially controlling and fuelled with power. If we use our previous argument that it is the emotional journey of a character which purveys the *true* sense of story, and that this story (premise, controlling idea) is rhetorical in intent, we can claim that the emotional journey is ideological. One example is *The Wizard of Oz*, where Dorothy's emotional journey comes to a climax when she returns to Kansas and rejoins her family, grateful to see them and wishing never to leave home again. Her words 'There's no place like home' serve not only her character happiness, but add to a potential reading of America as supreme country, the American dream as utopian ideal, and being true to and 'serving' the country by investing one's time, love and money there, rejecting invitations to 'go abroad' and mix with non-Americans (as symbolised by the Munchkins.) There are ways of challenging closure perhaps, but do non-ideological narratives or rejections of narrative pleasure actually work? The resolution could be seen as very dissatisfying if it fails to tie-up loose ends, return the characters to their normal world, or offer closure and catharsis for the audience. Thus, if a writer wants to experiment with closure, they have to bear in mind it is usually a high-risk venture.

11   Visual Storytelling

Potential speculations surrounding visual storytelling are numerous. One could indulge in a semiotic study of the signs and motifs on screen and assess their ideological function; or undertake an in-depth interrogation of a drama's use of mise-en-scène and draw alternative readings of meaning from various cultural and societal perspectives. Although these theories may prove useful for the screenwriter, enabling them to locate their art within a theoretical framework, we would like to focus on critical notions of visual storytelling linked directly to screenwriting practice. Debating notions which are deemed 'academic' are necessary in this section, but only when specifically connected with processes and reflections upon the art of writing.

Visual pleasure

This book speaks considerably about the notion of narrative pleasure. Stories are plotted in ways which appeal to audience emotions and expectations, possessing within them paradigms, sequences, turning points and narrative triggers which combine to form a holistic, pleasurable experience. The inference is that screenwriting assumes a commercial agenda, making the most of dramatic tools in order to appeal to the biggest audience. Visually speaking, we can develop a similar understanding. If the world is becoming more visually sophisticated and more eager to consume 'the look,' then screenwriting is perhaps one of the major contributing factors to this. Unlike classical dramas which would contain long dialogue-driven scenes, film and increasingly television today advances at breakneck speed with few scenes lasting more than two minutes, and most lasting less than one. The audience has become a visual expert, and more than this, hungry for visual pleasure over language. Jumping out of a burning aeroplane or skiing over the edge of a cliff is no longer seen as innovative, awe-inspiring action; it is the norm. Film-makers today have the burden of constantly trying to find the next big look, and screenwriters have to understand this shift and, if aiming for commercial success, incorporate it into their work.

That said, the sensory 'ride' that visual pleasure offers is highly alluring. Though visual spectacle is often the privileged playground of high budget Hollywood, it is possible to work with the concept of the sensory ride in terms of the emotional arc, and recently many films opt for smaller palettes, creating depth of drama rather than visual spectacle. Thus it is about discovering the right tone for a story, and understanding what makes a production possible (see Chapter 13).

Visual spectacle

Geoff King suggests that film (and television) spectacle 'offers a range of pleasures associated with the enjoyment of 'larger than life' representations, more luminous or intense than daily reality' (2000: 4). In essence, audiences sit in front of a screen and expect to see a step beyond reality; bigger and better than something they have experienced themselves. Action films have traditionally been associated with visual excess, sight and spectacle taking precedence over story and emotion. This is still often the case with action adventure films still pushing for the 'next best look,' but visual spectacle and sophistication is no longer limited to this genre. That is to say, visual spectacle is no longer tied solely to the visual elements of the screen (location, costume, movement). As Chapter 10 has shown, screenwriters are increasingly aware of alternative, non-linear methods of storytelling which in many cases encapsulate the idea of the visual spectacle. Parallel stories, for example, are based upon the assumption that the audience will possess the sophistication to make links between the interwoven narratives presented, and often the way these narratives are spliced together creates a heightened visual experience. In *The Hours*, the opening sequence which frames the three stories is a visual spectacle in itself, not like a *James Bond* movie with giant vistas infiltrated with chases, fights and explosions, but a spectacle created by the pace, camera movement and scene transitions which bind the three time frames together. Similarly with *Paris, Je T'aime*, although individually many of the films do not employ spectacular visual sequences (though there are some), collectively the film offers a sense of spectacle in presenting eighteen different worlds with eighteen different directors. Moving from film to film, the audience is invited to participate in a series of visual worlds connected by their very contrasting nature. Collectively, they provided an 'MTV style' experience of short, segmented narratives suitable for modern short attention spans.

Visual spectacle then should, for the screenwriter, be understood as a concept of invoking the audience into the narrative and offering a heightened experience of the eye. This does not solely necessitate the use of big explosions and camera tricks, but can be created by narrative experimentation. In fact, as King asserts, '[s]pectacle is often just as much a core aspect of Hollywood cinema as coherent narrative and should not necessarily be seen as a disruptive intrusion from some place outside' (Ibid.). What this means is that rather than view visual spectacle as a separate entity devised for instant audience gratification, it can be linked to elements of film-making such as narrative structure. For the screenwriter, this creates an awareness of how visual spectacle can be employed within the screenplay with a *function* rather than just for a *fashion*.

King offers an analysis of some of the 'traditional' elements of spectacle employed in *The Last Kiss Goodnight* (Ibid.: 91–4). He discusses how the audience is pulled into the film's scenes, the experimental editing and 3D-style audience perspective creating a heightened sense of reaction and interaction. His subtitle notes how quite literally the film offers 'a series of blows to the consciousness and emotions of the audience.' This is interesting because it suggests that although the spectacular scenes give visual appeal, they also invoke psychological attachment. Spectacle is thus an experience of emotion as well as one of vision, once more highlighting that the screenwriter's concerns with narrative are embodied in a wider, critical understanding of visual storytelling. A more recent trilogy of films serves this argument well: *The Bourne Identity*, *The Bourne Supremacy* and *The Bourne Ultimatum*. Although these films are spectacular in their experimentation with the 'look' and 'feel' of a scene, the camera adopting documentary-style aesthetics and heavy use of chases, fights and explosions, through this they offer a deep understanding of character and narrative journey. Car chases, rooftop fights and plunges from skyscrapers are not simply there to fuel visual expectation; they fulfil emotional experience. The over-arching story of the trilogy is the desperate attempt by protagonist Jason Bourne to find out who he really is and work out why the CIA is trying to kill him. For the audience this is the real substance of the films, the pinnacle of dramatic need and character motivation. Therefore, when the audience is taken on a camera ride of thrills, spills and motion sickness, they are also taken on a ride of desperation and passion. The psychosomatic effects of the visual spectacle are aligned with the narrative of Jason Bourne. The audience is put in his place, chased around the world and forced to make quick, sharp decisions.

The sheer determination of the CIA to kill him, and his own unknow-ingness about why this is, is depicted by the camera. Therefore, as well as offering an array of visual delight, the films offer a tumultuous jour-ney of a naïve, desperate individual. Even the flashbacks Bourne expe-riences, reminding him momentarily of his past, are narrative drives as well as (if not more than) visual spectacles. Although they may satisfy an audience's craving for stimulating visual aesthetics, they crucially serve to piece together the narrative drive of the films; memory and a reconciliation of it.

We can therefore argue that visual spectacle can be repositioned for those whose interests lie within screenwriting. Although on the one hand notions of screen spectacle can be argued as excess, not necessar-ily pertaining to narrative intentions and somewhat disrupting the flow of a plot, conversely it can be argued for a reiteration of narrative, one which makes an attempt to visually represent emotion. These specu-lations are perhaps vulnerable to those whose concerns are different, visual theoreticians, for example, but when considering screenwriting as a site of knowledge they make absolute sense; the value of such criti-cal insight comes in how this information is applied in practice. For the screenwriter working to deepen their knowledge and understanding of the discipline, an interrogation of visual spectacle can certainly offer alternative, usable possibilities.

Visual consumption

It is not only the look and pleasure of the film that is important for contemporary audiences. To extend the pleasure of the drama, both visually and to some extent narratively, production companies actively seek ways of exploiting the 'brand' of the story and forcing it into other areas of popular culture:

> in an age in which the big Hollywood studios have become absorbed into giant conglomerates, the prevalence of spectacle and special effects has been boosted by a growing demand for products that can be further exploited in multimedia forms such as computer games and theme-park rides.

> (Ibid.: 2–3)

Thus, the pleasure of a drama goes beyond the traditional screen. If the advent of video, DVD and published screenplays can be called *secondary texts*, then concepts like the computer game, theme park ride and even everyday products (wallpaper, socks, diary, birthday card) can be termed *hyper texts*. They are visually driven products or services no longer confined within the realms of a screen, but allowing a fantasy of character ('being Jack Sparrow') and re-experiencing of the world ('pirates on boats') to invade everyday life and blur boundaries between fact and fiction, life and drama. In some cases it even becomes unclear which 'text' came first: the film or the book? Did they make the *Pirates of the Caribbean* theme park ride because of the film, or was the film made because of the success of the ride? On the surface these may seem like bizarre questions, but they are a condition of contemporary life. Culture is obsessed with the appeal of the look, with instant recognition of a type, of verisimilitude, so it is perhaps no wonder the look of a film or TV drama is dispersed into everyday culture. Ironically, this places subsequent demands from the audience who, because they have become so used to visual culture and product offered by such texts, now expect more of it to be rearticulated in the original text. For example, if a computer game released after a film allows interactivity and offers new perspectives of character and world, any follow-up film to the original will have to incorporate this. If an audience can gain more visual pleasure out of the game than the new film, it is likely the new film will flop. The new film will have to 'better' the game, adopting perhaps even newer visual techniques, aiming to pull in the audience hungry for more with each text. These speculative debates about visual pleasure are not allied to every audience demographic and to every genre, but are seen as pervasive models. For a screenwriter working on a relevant project, these debates are paramount. Visual pleasure is all around us, and epitomised by film and television. Whether a product of or a producer of the ever-increasing need for visual satisfaction, screenwriting must face up to the challenge.

Advanced visual production techniques and animation

The rise of CGI (Computer Generated Imagery) has enabled the screenwriter to enter whole new territories, making scripts more akin to prose fiction in that the imagination can run riot. Screenwriters are no longer tied to naturalism or what is possible in practice. The ultimate expression of this is writing for animation, where the screenwriter can completely abandon the real and any concerns of what may or may not be possible on screen (beyond the costs of animating it).

As screenwriting, the story still has to be expressed mainly in visual terms, but like a novel, it allows the writer's imagination to roam free and create any world they like. This fantasy aspect of cinema has been a surprisingly long standing element and the development of visual (VFX) and special effects (SFX) can be seen as the struggle to make the invisible visible; to allow the audience the pleasure of seeing what normally resides in the imagined. This is a powerful subconscious aspect of cinema-as-spectacle, and screenwriters can be instrumental in shaping these visual experiences, far more so than special effects supervisors, directors and animators, as the writing is where it is imagined.

Since visual effects tend to be expensive, such storytelling often has to veer towards the commercial to recoup the financial outlay. However, it is possible for independent productions to create low-budget CGI, as these techniques are now in the hands of 'bedroom producers', just like DV cameras and editing software. In this way the imagination really is the only limit and screenwriters can begin to embrace the visual possibilities of the digital age; see Chapter 14 for an accompanying exercise.

The sound–image relationship

Although screenwriting is discussed as a predominantly visual medium, some of the most powerful emotive experiences and memorable storytelling moments are enabled through the use of sound. Indeed, sound can be seen as the *unconscious* of cinema, whereby visuals carry surface meaning and content, and music and sound design create the emotional and sensory container through which that content can be mediated. The presence and impact of sound is often invisible to audiences, but nevertheless richly experienced; the invisible thread connecting them to the felt story.

Screenwriters are often told not to include direct references to songs or pieces of music in a script, this being a producer, director and sound supervisor role (soundtracks have huge potential costs and associated marketing issues). What is 'allowed' is if there is one specific piece of music associated with a particular character that plays a central narrative role (such as ABBA songs in *Muriel's Wedding*), and must be included for the story to work. Any more than this is usually seen as a mark of amateur writing. However, screenwriters can embrace sound rather than music as a highly useful tool in writing scene action. Sound creates much of the resonance and atmosphere for a scene, and though it is difficult to replicate on the page, a skilled writer can suggest evocative sounds at key moments to provide subtle, sophisticated storytelling. Consider the following:

> Katy sits ensconced in the warm café. Outside sirens wail, and the rain pours down. Footsteps rush past the window. Katy lifts her coffee and sips slowly.

In this scene, images and non-dialogue sound combine to create an evocative mood (warmth) and sense of world (safe) that deepens the reader's understanding of the character's internal state (ease), and may also provide rhythm and plot expectation. It is worth considering how a sound fits into the world or moment of the scene: is it intrusive or ignored; familiar or surprising; dramatic or reassuring? Sound is particularly useful in suspense genres, and all types of comedy, where they add not only atmosphere but a sense of rhythm and narrative structure. Sound should be used sparingly in a script, but in the right place can be a valuable asset to tone, world, character and subtext. Sound is a surprisingly relevant discussion within visual storytelling because in the screenwriter's craft, the two are closely connected and non-dialogue sound is expressed through visual scene action.

12   Dialogues   and   Voices

Working with voiceover

Many screenwriting texts warn against the use of voiceover, for a variety of good reasons. However, it is not voiceover itself that can be damaging, but rather the way it is employed. Novice writers often resort to it because their visual storytelling is not strong enough. Filled with awkward exposition it stops flow and *interrupts the drama*, pulling the audience out of the viewing experience. Though voiceover should be used with caution, it does possess many possibilities if used with purpose and skill. The secret of effective voiceover lies in the *added value* it brings; if it simply repeats what is already on screen or tries to provide factual information, the audience may feel they are being addressed by the writer rather than involved in the character. Writers need to be aware of the voiceover *function*. Who is speaking and what is the audience's relation to this narrative voice; can we trust it? Many Coen Brothers films, such as *The Big Lebowski* and *Blood Simple*, offer introductory voiceovers, often ironic in style, to set tone, character, world and theme. The story is contextualised through stating the theme, also true of *Magnolia*, where the unknown narrator offers audiences a way to interpret the coming events. In this way, introductory voiceovers can offer a thematic perspective to experience the story through an invitation to connect with the world.

As a type of dialogue, voiceover is closely connected to character. The danger when writing voiceover is that the writer uses it to impart fact in their own voice; when voiceover is imbued with character, it is more evocative and gains dramatic value. A deceptively simple example is *Veronique* (winner of the Orange FilmFour Prize for Short Film, 2002), in which a boy gives a tenderly comic account of his first love. One day on his regular bus journey to school, a beautiful girl appears and he falls head over heels in love. During the next few days he waits for her tirelessly, tries to pluck up courage to say hello, experiences bitter disappointment as his plans are thwarted, and ecstatic joy as she sits next to him. Then she mysteriously disappears; he never sees her again.

As the drama unfolds, the boy recounts the events to a friend in voice-over. Not only is it clearly in character, but also in counterpoint to the images. In the voiceover, the boy boasts of his amazing affair, how in love they were, how she was forced to leave. When combined with the images, the audience realises the fantasy: the visual reality shows he is nervous, gawky and unsuccessful in his amorous advances. Two different world views are thus provided, and it is through their collision that richness of meaning, humour and emotional experience is created.

If a script needs voiceover, writers must decide how words and images should work together; how they add to or contrast with each other. It is important to consider who is talking and the trustworthiness of their voice, who they are talking to and why. All these elements affect the *status of truth* within voiceover, and transform it from dry, factual recounting to communication filled with dramatic tension, subtext and character.

Screenwriting and authorship

The screenwriter has been somewhat neglected from the canon of screen theory to date, much in-depth analysis focussing upon the role of the director as 'front runner'. While this may be true to a certain extent, many directors becoming synonymous with their productions,[1] the role of the screenwriter should not be ignored. Without a script there is no drama; without a writer, there is no director. As John Caughie outlines, art is an expression of the individual artist's emotions, experiences and world views (2001: 10), and although this view has come to be associated with the director, whose vision allegedly drives the production, we would like to argue that the same can be said of the screenwriter. Screenwriters too draw upon 'artistic' inspiration to drive the stories they tell. They are not merely creative technicians who perform the mechanical duties of writing a screenplay, but creative writers who draw upon personal emotions, expressions and world views. Thus, although most screen theory points towards the role of the director, we would like to reposition it in order to value the role of the screenwriter; their authorial voice and vision.

Caughie provides useful insights into the notion of *auteurism*, steeped firmly in the status of the film director. He proposes some basic assumptions:

> a film, though produced collectively, is most likely to be valuable when it is essentially the product of its director ... a film is more than

likely to be an expression of [the director's] individual personality; and that this personality can be traced in a thematic and/or stylistic consistency over all (or almost all) the director's films.

(Ibid.: 9)

What is interesting about these assumptions, widely accepted in the realm of film and television studies, is that they can be argued to make no sense at all. Why, for example, would a film be more likely to express the director's personality when she has not written the screenplay? Why would a TV drama be more valuable because of its director and not its writer? If mise-en-scène is viewed as an important tool for directing a sense of authorship (Ibid.: 12–13), the director writing their style via the camera's position, movement and look of the frame, then where in this does the story fare? Since what grips an audience to a story is its theme, structure and characters, it stands to reason that the screenwriter can be equally, if not more, valued as *auteur*. The notion of *authorial voice* in film is certainly intricate, as Tariq Anwar explains:

> In story terms the film that's screened or televised is assumed by reviewers and audiences to have always been that way. The fact that scenes may have been deleted and rearranged will not be apparent. The fact that shots have been re-framed, re-graded or digitally enhanced will also go unnoticed. Maybe an actor's performance is improved through judicious cutting or in post-synching, or a point made more clear by editing for overlaid ADR [automatic dialogue replacement] lines.
>
> (quoted in Perkins and Stollery, 2004: 27)[2]

There are thus a number of production roles which could assume the role of author, each striving to be the voice of the piece. If we do take the screenwriter as author, however, even this is complex. A script may not purely be single-authored; rather, as discussed in Chapter 8, the development process often sees a number of people (credited or uncredited) working on the same script. This posits the notion that screenwriting cannot be seen to have one author (or auteur), but a set of authors working collaboratively for the same cause. However, some screenwriters do express their personalities enough that they create a traceable voice throughout their work.

Andrew Spicer offers an interesting account of British screenwriter Richard Curtis, a figure 'whose reputation has been gained entirely through his screenwriting' (2007: 89). His article highlights how Curtis has restored the role of the screenwriter, audiences knowing the type of film on offer upon hearing his name alone. Through successes like *Four Weddings and a Funeral, Bean, Notting Hill* and *Love Actually*, Curtis has become a 'brand' which (for some) guarantees audience satisfaction; or at least, audience familiarity. Spicer outlines how Curtis's partnership with Working Title has played a crucial role in his career, hooking into and delivering the company's ethos of creating 'stylish, commercial films aimed at a maturing yuppie audience, and upbeat enough to play on both sides of the Atlantic' (Tim Bevan, quoted in Spicer, 2007: 93–4). What is interesting about Curtis is the role he takes in the life of a film, responsible not only for idea creation and screenplay but seeing the project through to editing (and in the case of *Love Actually*, being the director). Spicer is careful to warn against replacing the role of the director (auteur) with the role of the screenwriter, choosing instead to detail the collaborative process that filmmaking entails but with a focus upon the screenwriter (Ibid.: 89–90). Although this is a valid comment, we could argue that the screenwriter *can* in fact replace the role of the director as auteur. It is precisely Curtis's stylistic and thematic tendencies that make him an auteur, consistently presenting feel-good screenplays set in middle-class environments, focussing upon bumbling heroes and glamorous (often American) heroines. Inspired by his own life and cultural surroundings, Curtis's work is a representation of him: an artistic expression of his emotions, experiences and world views, as Caughie would have it. He is certainly viewed as one of Britain's leading screenwriters, in commercial terms anyhow, and is reliant upon the brand he has created in order to sustain this position. Sometimes it is the ensemble of cast, but overall the screenwriting that marks Curtis and his work; tone, humour, theme, situation, environment. This even extends into the secondary screenwriting market of DVD commentaries and published screenplays, as 'Curtis's name, very unusually for a writer, is used in marketing and promotion and his role is commented on extensively in reviews' (Ibid.: 100).[3]

Julia Hallam writes that '[a]uthorial innovation rather that generic renovation is the keystone of 'quality' drama' (2000: 141), a view which supports the premise that the screenwriter can be assigned the role of auteur. Whether via style of writing (voice) or profile of writing (ideas), the quotation goes some way in recognising that screenwriters can portray themselves through their work. Rib Davis alludes to authorial voice in his discussion of writers such as David Hare, Arthur Miller, Caryl Churchill and David Mamet (2003: 89).[4] He outlines how they are distinctive writers who write beyond 'real life' and naturalism. Their styles and quirks of writing offer a sense of heightened reality, and for the audience, a heightened experience of the spoken word. They are writers who purvey a sense of authorial voice that, although confined to generic or commercial constraints, breaks out and stands up for itself and its creator. One other writer we wish discuss is Jonathan Harvey, a British screenwriter who has worked extensively in film and television over the last fifteen years. Harvey's big break came with award winning film *Beautiful Thing*, originally written for stage but adapted for the screen in 1996. This film is central to Harvey's voice as it characterises an important theme running throughout his work: homosexuality. Not only do many of his projects involve themes of gay men and gay life-styles (his signature body of work), they also offer a distinct sense of a 'gay voice'; camp, ballsy, rhythmical and lovingly bitchy.

Harvey created and wrote BBC sitcom *Gimme, Gimme, Gimme*, based around struggling gay actor Tom Farrell (James Dreyfus) and layabout 'fag hag' Linda La Hughes (Kathy Burke). Needless to say, much of the humour was derived from the ultra-camp Tom and his relationship with Linda, the use of observation and cliché surrounding homosexu-ality suggesting it could only have been written by a gay man. This was followed-up in 2005 with another sitcom concept, *Love for Sale*, part of the BBC's *Last Laugh* competition. Only one pilot episode was written, but nevertheless bore all the hallmarks of Harvey:

> A sitcom set in a gay escort agency from a bungalow in suburbia. The loudmouthed proprietress, Bo-Jangles Hart, is a 42 year old pre-operative transsexual. Hard drinking and self obsessed, Bo is a mother hen who would do anything for 'her boys'.
>
> (from the BBC's *Last Laugh* website)

Harvey's sexuality seems to influence his writing heavily: the concept, characters and even subplot focus upon a gay world. In 2004 he wrote *Von Trapped*, a one-off comedy drama for ITV about one woman's obsession with *The Sound of Music* and her dream of being like Julie Andrews. The cultural importance of *The Sound of Music*, read here as a motif of gay life and gay tastes, posits the drama firmly in Harvey's domain. Another drama appropriating Harvey's inspiration from gay life is *Charlie's Angel*, part of the BBC's 2004 *Twisted Tales* season which explores the developing love affair between two young men/ghosts. In sum, we can see that Harvey's profile clearly purveys his individualistic sense of identity and taste. The types of stories he tells and the charac-ters that drive them are essentially experiences from his personal life and demonstrators of a world or culture in which he lives.

One of the most interesting case studies to evidence authorial voice is Harvey's work on *Coronation Street*, which he joined in 2004. Typically, soap opera is the least likely source for authorial voice. It is a producer-led, mass-made form which usually denies any sense of ownership for individual episodes. What has become apparent in Harvey's case is that though writers are working to tight storylines and are at the eventual mercy of a script editor, he still manages to purvey his own sense of voice and, arguably, episode ownership. This is not to say other writers are not capable of the same,[5] but knowing Harvey's extensive work and personality from other dramas, the audience can hear his voice. One way he achieves this is by consistent references to popular gay icons and artists: Danny La Rue, Sheena Easton, Dusty Springfield. Even though the characters are not specifically talking about these people, the story beat not requiring their mention, they are cleverly and credibly inserted to add humour and a gentle camp-ness. Other moments of camp humour are used throughout a variety of episodes to invite the audience to participate in the almost self-conscious world of Harvey. Examples include references to clutch bags, pan scrubs, wigs, thermal vests, and Blanche's story of Deirdre as a child, standing with a tea towel on her head playing 'Once in Royal David's City' in C Major. It can be said that such references, influenced by a strong sense of effeminate humour, act as an interplay of verbal signs and motifs which brand the humour as belonging to Harvey. *Coronation Street* itself is often described as a camp, surreal world compared to *EastEnders*, for example, but what Harvey does is take this one step further into exaggerated realm of theatrics; even pantomime. Gareth Philips is a former script editor for *Coronation Street*, and when interviewed did confirm that 'fluidity and freedom of creative expression' are always encouraged with the show's writers. Even though each episode has a strict storyline, the writing process is organic and individual voices shine through. As detailed in the case of Jonathan Harvey, his personal life and social world form a strong part of his writing. His signature style does not reside in the look of the scene or movement of the camera, as predicated by the history of screen studies, but lies in his ability to create worlds and stories around themes and ideas close to his heart. For the aspiring or even working screenwriter, this concept should be embraced. Story types and voices should be developed effectively and with pride so we can finally begin, as Andrew Spicer's chapter title suggests, to restore the screenwriter to film (and television) history.

Authorial voice as marketing tool

Questions of voice are useful for writer consideration when finding a niche in the marketplace and offering a 'USP' (Unique Selling Point), yet it is seldom reflected upon. It could be argued that as screenwriting gives the author less status, there is less need for the writer to be an 'artist' rather than 'craftsperson', but this we feel is short-sighted. Producers, especially in television, often proclaim to be on the look out for 'fresh original voices,' and even in Hollywood, writers are hired to polish existing scripts because of a particular talent, be it dialogue, action sequences or comedy. As such this can be seen to offer the USP of voice, distinguishing one writer from another. Though this is 'voice-as-skill' rather than 'voice-as-author', we would argue it still defines and empowers writers. It can thus be very helpful to consider the particular features of a voice, what tastes and passions make a writer unique, and find a way to offer this writing identity to producers.

Novice writers often aim too wide. They sometimes have little idea of what distinguishes television writing from feature film, think little about what type of story they enjoy, and when sending out work do so indiscriminately, with little research into which producer or production company might be most suitable. Agents also find it difficult to work with a writer when they have no sense of what career path they want to follow. This is not to say a writer has to restrict their options; they simply have to be more aware of them. Some writers want to write for soaps, some for children; some love television crime series, some want to focus exclusively on horror features or subtle human drama. What we argue is not that writers shape themselves to the market, but rather become aware of their strengths, talents and *writing pleasures*, then use them to clarify the most fitting career path. If a writer is more specific about their creative goals, both agents and producers become more inspired and assured, and opportunities increase. It is not enough to want to be a screenwriter; instead, writers need to consider what kind of screenwriters they are or want to be. Thousands of writers exist, so how does a producer select a particular writer for a job? The spec script is only a very small part of the writing market and jobs mainly come from commission or adaptations (see Chapter 1). Apart from solid craft skill, it is the writer's voice, their USP, that plays a vital part in being selected for a job – that, and tireless social networking.

Writing in a writer's voice rather than a character's can, however, be tricky. With dialogue, good practice is nearly always to adopt the language of individual characters, but there are some who find a way to blend the two. An obvious example is Quentin Tarantino, who applied his own high-octane motormouth to characters with great success. This was a fresh voice seldom heard, confident and in tune with character, theme and world; the exception that proved the rule. However, most authorial styles are not so clear-cut, and finding one's voice can be difficult. The writer's voice is not only expressed through dialogue and style of writing, but also in the ideas and thematic territory making up the body of work. For many writers, the stories they tell and issues they explore are the mark of their professional personality. Often a writer is not aware of the elements that define their voice, and paradoxically if they become too self-aware of them, they can lose their impact. Thus, a writer's voice is often best discovered upon reflection rather than pursued on purpose; that is, by writing instinctively, then looking back at what has been produced. Setting-out to create a specific 'voice' can end up sounding forced, fake and hollow. It is far preferable to allow it to evolve organically by writing, then reflecting on where the real skills and desires of the voice lie. This is what makes voice both unique and a selling point, helping producers realise why one writer is more suitable to a project than another.

13   Further   Cultures   of   Screenwriting

This chapter will explore some emerging and changing cultures of screenwriting, and ways that writers can shape their careers in more unconventional ways. The industry is constantly evolving and screenwriters need to keep abreast of developments, but as with all systems, cracks exist and writers can subvert and challenge current practices if they are willing to work hard and push creative boundaries.

Commercial vs commercially viable

As argued in Chapter 6, screenwriting is the form of creative writing most closely allied to business rather than art. This does not mean the only road to success is through high-concept Hollywood, but it does mean screenwriters must understand the realities of film financing and production. Central to this debate is the concept of commercial vs commercially viable scripts. A *commercial* script appeals to a large audience and makes a large sum of money. Examples include sequels (*James Bond, Batman*), adaptations (*Harry Potter, Lord of the Rings*) and high-concept ideas (*Meet the Parents, The 40 Year Old Virgin*). A *commercially viable* script earns more money than it costs to make, however small its audience. Embracing this difference enables screenwriters to grasp the impact of challenging conventions and creating stories outside the norm. Considering how to make a script commercially *viable*, rather than simply commercial, empowers the writer to make informed choices. For instance, if a horror premise seems 'art house' in style and theme, to boost the chances of production the writer could either revise it as high-octane slasher action, or reduce the special effects and make it work on a small budget. Such restrictions can actually encourage creativity, and should be viewed by writers as opportunities to expand ideas and techniques. A smaller budget allows for more risks and experimentation; a larger budget usually insists on relatively conventional practice, and by considering this during idea stage and script development, writers can fashion the stories they want and still have a possibility of selling them.

Cultures of production and distribution

Over the last ten years, marked changes in cinematic production have led to alternative filmmaking and screenwriting cultures, challenging and transforming the mainstream. Digital technology such as mini-DV cameras and laptop editing software has made production far more accessible and it is now possible to make a digital feature on a very low budget. Independent productions abound, with financial control redistributed towards producers rather than financiers. Audiences do not always welcome the unconventional, however, and filmmakers have to bear in mind how to connect to them. Danish Dogme95 films such as *Festen* convinced audiences to accept new technical conventions of low visual quality (digital, hand-held, unlit) through assured, high-quality storytelling. These films actively prioritise story, often through actor–director collaboration rather than traditional scripting (see Chapter 8). Whether low budget or not, they spend their funds on story and character rather than technology and spectacle, providing a stark contrast to recent Hollywood focus and suggesting a desire for 'real' as opposed to 'manipulated' emotion. For Peter Schepelern, the main aim of Dogme95 was to 'combat predictable plots, superficial action and cosmetic technological trickery' (n.d.,: para 3); and Thomas Vinterberg, creator of *Festen*, agrees: 'I wanted to counter the mediocrity and the conventional ... Dogme95 is my attempt to undress film, to reach the 'naked film'' (n.d: FAQ).

It is now possible for writers and filmmakers to script and produce a feature film without conceding control and attempt to sell their product not as script but as film. This means distributors buy finished product rather than investing in a script with potential but no certain quality, and allows writers and filmmakers more opportunity to experiment; they can let the finished material speak for itself rather than convince financiers of the value of a risky script. However, for writers, networking is always essential whether at conventional or grass-roots level, as directors and producers are required to turn work into saleable products. Recent changes in media technology and Internet communities such as Shooting People are transforming this process, allowing independent filmmakers to network in radical ways and form their own cultures of production (see Chapter 8). There are pitfalls, however, especially with regards to story. Easy-access technology can result in 'point-and-shoot' filmmaking, where record buttons are pressed with little thought for creative preparation. Often such filmmakers have little experience of screenwriting craft, and the quality of storytelling, structure and pace can be poor. This does not necessarily mean that current conventions of script development have to remain in place, but it does mean writers have to fight for their rightful place in the process, and insist on their value as expert craftspeople and storytellers.

The next evolutionary phase promising the possibility of change regards distribution. Every year, many films are made without ever reaching an audience and cinema in particular is heavily controlled by distributors, sales agents and exhibitors, who often decide not only which films are screened but also which scripts are produced. With huge sums ploughed into *P&A* (prints and advertising), smaller independent productions find it hard to fight for theatrical screen space. What may create a sea change is when digital distribution finally finds its feet, and the Internet becomes an accepted distribution channel for direct producer-to-audience communication. This is already happening to some extent, with sites such as *You Tube* and independent filmmakers selling DVDs online, and as witnessed in the music business, new technology can have a huge impact on the way industry is run. The same is likely to happen with film, including potential new platforms such as mobile phones and MP3 players. What remains to be seen is how writers and producers will use these new opportunities in terms of content, and whether audiences are as willing to embrace new forms of storytelling as they are new forms of technology.

Creating your own culture: Writers' groups

As discussed in Chapters 6 and 8, one of the key proficiencies of a screenwriter is working with others. Film and television is such a competitive environment; it is seldom conducive to mistakes, and producers work with writers they know will deliver. One way novice writers can gain experience is to join writers' groups, allowing them to analyse scripts, network and receive feedback in a safe place before sending work into the less forgiving industry. Paradoxically, because groups allow writers to hear the reactions of a number of readers simultaneously, it helps to clarify what are real story problems and what is merely personal taste. A mutually beneficial and supportive environment, a writers' group can be a productive, creative space but needs guidelines to run well:

(1) *Choose Members Carefully*. Crucial as a group's quality and energy comes down to this. Choose members of a similar standard or similar place in their writing careers, who want roughly the same thing. Although every member does not have to turn up to every meeting, it is essential everyone is committed, not only to the group but to the work and each other.

(2) *Limit Numbers*. Keep the group small to enable fruitful discussion and allow members to develop relationships with each other. 4–7 is good.

(3) *Device a General Strategy*. Useful as a first session and icebreaker. Discuss what members want from the group (script analysis, writing exercises, general support?) and how sessions will be structured; how long, how often etc.

(4) *Make it Regular*. Every 3–6 weeks is a good guideline to make members feel part of something with momentum. Any less and it can be difficult to stay engaged; anything more and people may have trouble attending regularly.

We would advice writers to embrace this grass-roots culture as it is highly useful in heightening both skill and building confidence. It is also useful for experienced writers as a space in which to play, experiment and create peer support, including sharing news and industry gossip as useful creative networking.

Cultures of teaching screenwriting

The teaching of screenwriting has in itself a distinct culture which is useful to analyse in order to challenge received notions and develop the field of study. Training screenwriters is big business and we would question underlying assumptions of what needs to be taught, how to become a writer and what 'good writing' is. A revealing approach is to compare the ideological concepts in screenwriting teaching to that of creative writing, both in Higher Education and in short-term workshops. Academically, creative writing is a far more established discipline whereas screenwriting is only beginning to make an impact. Although closely allied, creative writing is usually based in English Literature departments and screenwriting in Media and Film, which means historically they have developed separately. In broad terms, key differences are that in creative writing the writer is the 'author' and given high status, whereas in screenwriting the writer possesses lower status. In creative writing, the writer is seen as creator with spark and vision; in screenwriting, writers are often seen as 'mechanics' whose main tasks are to engineer, construct and refine story structure. In creative writing there is often a greater focus on 'creative preparation' such as finding and defining narrative voice and writing style, whereas in screenwriting there is an emphasis on 'technical preparation' such as pitching and plotting. The main *writing currency* in fiction is prose style, whereas the main currency in screenplays is structure. This means teaching is approached differently: for fiction, free-standing writing exercises are offered, focusing on language, metaphor, voice and description; screenwriting deals with acts, step outlines, cards and character arcs. Rewriting is often unstructured in fiction, seen as flowing naturally from the writer, whereas in screenwriting it is distinct, substantial and essential, engaging with disciplined drafts and embracing feedback. Fiction writing is often seen as a solitary act by an independent author, whereas screenwriting is viewed a business, requiring understanding of genre, pitching and production. Finally, the fiction writer delivers a finished piece of work, whereas screenwriters are dependent on filmmakers to reach the audience.

Comparing these related disciplines, it becomes obvious that the two can learn from each other, whether in a formal teaching context or as writers' own practice. Screenwriting could offer fiction writing ways to work with structural planning and plotting, a more productive rewrite process, strong analytical and editing skills and engaging with the marketplace. Fiction writing could offer screenwriting more focus on exploring creativity as a learned skill, the importance of daily writing practice and exploring authorial voice. We would thus challenge the present ideology of a large proportion of screenwriting training which focuses on the 'mechanics' of the form rather than aligning it with creative practices successfully used in other forms of writing, and strongly recommend a more productive exchange between disciplines.

Changing cultures of genre

In the global market of fierce competition and profit margins, distributors increasingly appeal to audience tastes by harnessing a sense of product need. This is none more evident than in the desire for consuming genre and a growing wave of films such as *Scary Movie* (and its sequels), *Date Movie*, *Epic Movie* and *Not Another Teen Movie* are adopting a genre label of *genre*. Spoof, parody, 'gross out' satires, their very nature points towards and mocks the Hollywood system of producing films according to genre, suggesting they are formulaic, follow stereotypical frameworks and share the same audiences. They can be seen to embody what television historian Michael Curtin calls 'innovation, imitation and saturation' (1995: 248, cited in Mittell, 2003: 48), a process whereby, in television as well as film, producers clone successful productions in order to gain large audiences who are 'least objectionable' to what they see. The new 'genre' genre not only epitomises this state in production ethic, but also takes it one step further by making the audience aware of how it operates. Taking the slasher genre, films like *Halloween*, *Scream* and *I Know What You Did Last Summer* are inspiration for *Scary Movie*, but this film does not just imitate them; it makes fun of them, acknowledging the system and mocking the films, those who make them and, to some extent, the audiences who pay to see them. In an interview, one of the film's creators, Marlon Wayans, discusses how the film works:

> As a parody, you have to take things to the ceiling. You can't go in-between. They have to see the joke. In taking it to the extreme sometimes you get caught out in the gross thing. But we don't want to be gross; we want to be funny. We're not "Porkies" or a teen comedy. We are a parody; which is a genre within itself.
>
> (quoted in Harris, 2001)

This is a recognition of the need to clarify what the joke is, in this case involving distinctive markers of the generic slasher conventions. Whether this is part of the structural form, character ensemble or visual grammar, the emphasis resides with highlighting the generic conventions to the audience and heightening them to a state of parody; a *mega narrative* is thus created which epitomises the whole genre. *Scary Movie* plays upon everything an audience knows about the slasher, 'a horror film in which isolated psychotic individuals (usually male) are pitted against one or more young people (usually females) whose looks, personalities, and/or promiscuities serve to trigger recollections of some past trauma in the killer's mind' (Schneider, 2000: 7, cited in Hutchings, 2004: 194). The narrative of a slasher is also reliant upon fears of sex and sexual violation, teenage angst and fear of the impending adult future (linked to rites of passage narratives), all brought out by the parody. Discussing the nature of the slasher, Peter Hutchings writes:

> Beforehand, shocks had tended to be placed firmly within, and subordinated to, particular narrative structures. In the slasher, however, the delivery of shocks seems to become the main point of the film, with the narratives organised around the shock sequences rather than the other way round.
>
> (2004: 206)

This points towards the particular narrative demands of genre (see Chapter 6), and *Scary Movie* recognises this pattern in the slasher, employing it in a sarcastic and somewhat demeaning tone which, nevertheless, tells the screenwriter a great deal about the genre in question; and how that genre can be written. *Date Movie* is similar in its parody of the romantic comedy, where all things that can go wrong on a date, will. *Epic Movie* takes intertextual references from high budget, lavish adventure stories where bravery, heraldry and long battles for justice prevail. For these reasons, genre films are a rich source of learning for screenwriters as well as a speculative area for critique; obviously stretched and exaggerated, they illuminate the power of genre and the way audiences relate to it.

Structures of reality TV

As a final point to the book, it is worth considering how, with the explosion of reality TV programming previously discussed, so-called factual shows are turning to screenwriting structures to inform their own telling; the blurring of fact and fiction. Has the concept of dramatic structure inherent in fictional drama seeped into contemporary factual and entertainment production? We believe that in many contemporary reality formats there is a clear insistence on following a dramatically emphasised character journey. Subjects (characters) are seen overcoming obstacles and hurdles to achieve a new balance in their life, looking back at the journey and assessing how they have grown during it. Shows such as *Wife Swap, Holiday Showdown, You Are What You Eat, What Not To Wear, Brat Camp*, even lifestyle programmes like *Location, Location, Location* and *Property Ladder*, are increasingly structured like film and TV drama. They are about emotions, journeys of self-discovery and lessons learned. They are driven by narrative structures not dissimilar to those like *The Wizard of Oz* and *Lord of the Rings*. As Holmes and Jermyn suggest, we are at a significant moment in broadcasting history where the form of the documentary has lost its original meaning and purpose. We can certainly see that a relocation of the traditional factual form, function and set of practices has 'fostered the creation of a proliferating and much extended space for the production and consumption of 'factual' programming which problematises documentary's (already contested) status' (2004: 2), and the creation of new genres of factual programming truly position the documentary as expandable, changeable, fluid and, arguably, unstable. It could thus be argued that these genres of hybrid show are diverting from traditional documentary 'truth' and instead using structure and character to create emotive, dramatic experiences. The programmes offer narratives about real people, geared towards a particular set of story outcomes. Whether learning to be a better mother, how to dress well or fit a bathroom, these programmes have core emotional drives and specific desired outcomes just like fictional drama. Laurie Hutzler writes that '[y]ou can only reach the universal through the personal' (2005: 8); that the universal appeal of drama is relayed via an individual's plot. These kinds of reality show do not actually tell individual stories, but use individual plots (via their subjects) to tell universal stories. Their meta-narratives appeal to a mass audience using the form of an individual subject.

In sum, strong connections can be made between fictional drama and contemporary reality TV; a constant blending and blurring of fact and fiction. Fact can inform fiction, but needs to be heavily reliant upon fiction in order to 'make sense.' Fiction can and does inform fact, making facts intelligible and pleasurable as a narrative. With this need for constant fictions, a 'storied world', we ask whether reality can ever exist, or is it always a dramatic representation? Will reality in fact become one big fiction as audiences progressively demand its narrative reformulation in order to be understood, digested and fully experienced? And if this is the world we live in, what is your story?

14 Key Points and Speculations Exercises

This final chapter illustrates key points covered in *Speculations,* and suggests exercises to develop a deeper understanding of them.

- **Exploring Possibilities**

Key point

A story is not always best served by having one sole author; collaboration can open up creativity and solid working relationships. Many forms of creative collaboration exist within screenwriting, from working with the feedback of script editors and producers, to team development and more innovative working practices.

Exercise: Creative collaboration

Devise a joint story-creation project either via the Internet or meeting in person. It may be team developing a TV series, co-writing a script, working with actors, or any other kind of collaborative work that allows a story to grow from shared rather than individual work. Write a brief project proposal document (one side of A4) so all contributors are clear on what is agreed, what the aims are and how long it will take. Once the work has been created, reflect on the process, writing 1–2 sides about how it felt to be a writer in this collaborative context, what the pros and cons were, how you would improve the working practice if you were to do it again and what you have learnt about writing through it. Share the reflections within your working group.

- ## Subjects: Ideas into Characters

Key point

Unlike fiction writers, screenwriters do not always train their creative writing muscle enough and this can lead to weak ideas and writer's block. It is important to make regular time for non-project work to develop craft. The following three exercises suggest ways of working with creativity; many more can be found in fiction writing books (such as Amanda Boulter's (2007) *Writing Fiction: Creative and Critical Approaches*).

Exercise: Words, bad and good

Write the letters of the alphabet at the top of a piece of paper – use one letter per page. Under each letter, list as many words as possible beginning with that letter. Try to list both verbs, nouns and adjectives. Keep going until the page is full, don't stop to think.

Once the page is done, read through the words and highlight ones you like, that interest or intrigue you or you like the sound of. Write a separate list of these, calling it 'good words'. Now pick out words you don't like – that you are frightened of, that make you uneasy or bored. Write a list of these, calling it 'bad words'. Use these lists to inspire you and mix 'good' and 'bad' words to see what creative sparks fly from their combinations.

Exercise: Observing a situation

Pick a situation to write about. It can be between two or more people, between one person and themselves, the environment or an object. Seek out a place where you are likely to find this situation happening. Alternatively, go to a specific location and see what situation catches your eye: a train station, library, sports event, a situation at home. Wherever you are, tune into 'writer mode' then observe the following:

- How are the people (or person and object/environment) interacting?
- Who has the power? How is the balance of power shifting and why?
- How are people expressing themselves? Details can be evocative, fresh and rich.

- Are there any tensions, spoken or unspoken? What is unsaid?
- How is one person trying to get another to do what they want?
- What do the various people want? Who is successful in getting it?
- How do they react to each other? What are the 'action – reaction – decisions' chains?

Exercise: Lists

Lists are a great creative tool as they really free the mind. There are many ways to use lists but a simple one is to write a list every day on a specific word. Choose a word, either one that pops into your mind or find one randomly in a dictionary, then write it at the top of a page. Write one hundred words that spring to mind from that one word. It does not matter if words are repeated, simply keep writing until you reach one hundred. You do not need to do anything with the list, it simply works to 'oil the brain', but if inspiration strikes you can use list words as the basis for a one hundred word screenplay premise.

Key point

Writers often settle on an idea too early, not fully exploring the possibilities it may hold. It is crucial not only to select the right idea, but to experiment and go beyond the obvious. Both the overall story and specific scene writing can benefit from finding fresher, more interesting ways to tell a familiar tale. Opposites are a powerful way to expand ideas and train the creative muscle and particularly useful for creating high-concept commercial ideas where you start with a familiar element and twist it (*Tootsie, Brokeback Mountain, Cars*).

Exercise: Using opposites to prod a premise

Create as many *opposite* versions of an idea as possible. Only change one aspect at a time, then another, until you have prodded every part for its possible opposite. One of these variations may not fully work in itself, but can help a writer open up and move beyond familiar terrain and flash up moments or variations that make a difference.

For instance, from the basic (rather dull and clichéd) premise: *Katrina is a shy secretary who longs for love but never goes out*, one could achieve the following versions by changing one aspect at a time into its opposite:

- PETER is a shy secretary who longs for love but never goes out.
- Katrina is a BOLSHY ARROGANT secretary who longs for love but never goes out.
- Katrina is a shy BOSS who longs for love but never goes out.
- Katrina is a shy secretary who IS SICK OF love and never goes out.
- Katrina is a shy secretary who longs for love and OBSESSIVELY ATTENDS SPEED DATING EVENTS.

Key point

Documentary dramas tell stories based on real people or events. They are constructed upon 'real life' but inevitably have to undergo some form of fictionalisation in order to work structurally. Understanding how *framing, focus, selection (persuasion)* and *resolution* work in a screenplay can help locate the central narrative intention of the drama (the aim) and provide understanding of how a writer has used narrative structure to tell a dramatic story derived from fact.

Exercise: Finding fiction within fact

Think about a person you know or know of, or research someone known to the general public. Begin to sketch a brief profile of how that person is or has been viewed. Are they liked or disliked? What have they achieved? Do they have any special talents? Now sketch a rough time-line of events that have occurred in their life, highlighting possible key moments that may provide dramatic potential.

Look at your material and ask yourself: can I find a story which would appeal to film or television audiences? The story may be obvious or may need teasing out; either way, make sure you draw from the reality of the person's life and not randomly make up big events. The main thing is to find a story which has a heart and will act as an underlying drive to any plot that takes place. This completed, work with the following framework to structure your story into a feature length drama.

- *Framing* – which event would provide the best opening sequence to hook an audience? How do you want the audience to feel about your character at the start? Which event(s) demonstrates this best? Is there something in the timeline that can be seen as a major event which posits the character in a dilemma, which is then overcome by subsequent plot? Why is *now* the best time to begin your character's story?

- *Focus* – which events should follow the opening sequence to allow for audience identification and reinforcement of the character's story? What could the inciting incident be? How should the inciting incident propel the character forward?

- *Selection (Persuasion)* – considering your central story, which events would best 'fit' your intentions? Do any of the real-life events have strong dramatic power which an audience would want to see? Which other characters might be introduced into the story to help or challenge your character? Are there any events or circumstances that do not happen, but which you think ought to in order to raise the dramatic potential?

- *Resolution* – how do you want the audience to feel about the character at the end of the drama? What emotions and viewpoints should the audience have in order for the story to work best? Are there any events which epitomise this or do you need to assert an amount of creative licence? How can the ending effectively link to the beginning, reinforcing themes and narrative intention?

Once you have researched a character and thought carefully about the questions above, you will have enough material to embark upon the creation of a documentary drama. The next stage may be to write a short outline, followed by a step outline or treatment.

Key point

A common way to make a genre feel fresh is finding a new world for the story to unfold in. This can also create a new mix of genres, which can prove commercial gold. There are two options: *put a familiar story into an unfamiliar world* (e.g. *Alien*) or *an unfamiliar story into a familiar world* (e.g. *Brokeback Mountain*). It is important to keep some degree of familiarity and not make every element unknown, as it helps give solidity to audience expectation and connection, and makes the idea saleable and attractive.

Exercise: Mixing genres and worlds

Choose an event, situation or character(s) and put them into a new environment to see how the characters react. What new situations are they forced to face or deal with? What helpful objects/characters/situations appear in this world? Does it make it funnier/scarier/more moving? Use your own combinations or choose from the prompts below. Note: here, the concept of 'world' is not used in the strict sense of location, but as a general situation to help the flow of ideas.

(1) Two people fall in love …
   • in a prison
   • by telepathy
   • through cooking
   • at a funeral
   • on a boat
   • from different sides of the world
   • from different parts of the universe
   • as animals
(2) Two people compete to find a secret object …
   • while in hospital
   • underground
   • while in an old people's home
   • in the last place on earth
   • as children
   • on a train
   • in space
   • in the stone age
(3) A character fights for survival …
   • at a zoo
   • in a marriage
   • during a balloon race
   • in an office
   • in a mysterious labyrinth
   • while riding an elephant
   • as a baby
   • in a forest

Creativity and freshness is often about new *combinations* rather than completely new ideas. The originality does not necessarily come from the building blocks themselves, but from how they are put together.

Key point

Screen characters can be understood more fully by an appreciation of character psychology. Going beyond basic steps in character creation (appearance, job, backstory), psychology can unearth crucial meaning to be transposed into the screenplay (childhood emotion, family relations, thwarted dreams.) Screenplays resonate with audiences to allow a sharing of emotional responses, and researching character psychology can enhance this by drawing upon ideas such as the shared unconscious and universal myth.

Exercise: Character psychology

Read Carl Jung on the *archetypes of character* (see Chapter 9), paying particular attention to notions of the hero and the shadow. Make notes about what each archetype embodies and how they are linked to wider ideas of psychology.

Now choose a film or TV drama you are familiar with and pay close attention to protagonist and antagonist; hero versus shadow. Write a synopsis of each character's 'story': who they are, what they want in life, why they are the way they are, what makes them tick. Try to write as if you are offering comparisons between the two characters, how the hero is different to the villain. Then put the two together and try to find common elements which bind the two characters; what is it that pulls the two together in the story? Are they really opposites or variants of the same character? Now look at a screenplay you are working on and ask the same questions. Do you learn anything new? Can you add any of this knowledge to the next stage of the screenplay's development?

- **Structures and Narratives**

Key point

Writers often settle on the structure of a story without having explored its alternatives. Since there are two layers to structure, plot (physical journey) and character arc (emotional journey), it is useful to experiment with different relationships and patterns between these. The same events can be fashioned into a totally different story depending on the *order* they come in. Whether it is done in a non-linear manner (see Chapter 10) or conventional structure, it is essential architectural exploration.

Exercise: Pushing structural boundaries

Using the following premise, attempt two exercises:

COLIN dreams of making it big as a magician but is crippled by shyness. Every time he tries to perform he starts to sweat and shake, his tricks go wrong and people laugh at him. Then one day he comes across something very special that may possibly grant him the success he dreams of – but at what price … ?

(1) Develop the premise into as conventional and commercial a three act structure as you can, using the quick *tent pole* method outlined in Chapter 3. Only write a sentence or two for each major beat to map out the whole arc without going into detail. This is about broad brushstrokes and essential architecture.
(2) Now take the same premise and write a non-linear story pattern. Keep to the same main events if you can but use an innovative structure to change the shape of the character journey, theme and audience experience. Use tentpoles rather than an outline to allow a clearer view of the architecture, then compare it with the conventional version. If you find it difficult to discover ways the same events might work in a different order, write each beat on an index card and lay them out to play with new combinations.

Once you have done both versions, reflect on what you learned about structure: what did you like, how did it make you think about structure and story and character, what possibilities did you begin to see in working with structure?

Key point

Closure is a crucial part of film and television. As well as bringing the story to a structural end, it gives the audience physical and emotional relief. Although non-traditional narrative structures may provide an audience with a different way of telling a story in the main, narrative closure is still usually desired. The ending does not have to be obvious or happy, but in some way needs to satisfy the appetite for cathartic closure. This is partly an ideological issue as it gives the audience a formulaic pattern of story, provides an emotional experience they are expecting and allows the screenwriter to use this as a way of dictating how the audience should accept the story.

Exercise: Finding closure

Choose a mainstream film and analyse its ending. Make notes about how it adheres to traditional notions of narrative closure. Now experiment with writing a different ending. Use extreme opposites where possible, such as the character dies instead of lives. Now test your alternative ending on other people. Ask these questions:

- What would your initial reaction be as an audience member?
- Would you feel satisfied with this different ending? If not, why not?
- Do you think the narrative works with the new ending, or would it need to be re-structured?
- What do you think an ending should include? Does this new one possess this, or is it lacking something?
- Which ending do you prefer, the old one or the new one? Why?

Use the answers and reactions to help you think about your work and how the ending may hold significant importance for audience satisfaction. If you want to be experimental and not offer traditional closure, use the responses to help you shape an ending which you think would be effective and relevant to the overall story and theme.

Key point

Reality TV is increasingly using screenwriting-style narratives to structure programmes. Subjects become characters, situations become story worlds, and facts become fictions. Looking at a full-length reality TV programme it is clear that a traditionally fictional narrative is working: problem, inciting incident, rising conflict, climax and resolution. Just like fiction, they have core emotional drives which resonate with the audience, from learning to be a better wife, to making a new life in the country.

Exercise: Faking it

Compare a reality TV show to a fictional drama, analysing how they share similar narrative structures and intentions. Think about the key points of plot in the reality TV show and how they relate to traditional storytelling (such as three act structure). Also consider how the subject of the show has been characterised for audience appeal. Key questions to respond to may include:

- Does the reality TV show have a clear *story* at its heart? What is it really about?
- Who are the main *characters* and how are they introduced?
- Does the presenter/narrator provide a sense of dramatic problem early on?
- Is there an inciting incident early in the show which sets the rest in motion?
- Can you identify rising tension and conflict?
- What are the hurdles and obstacles that are overcome?
- Do the characters reflect upon their *journey* and learn anything from it?
- What is the core emotional value that the show tries to present?

- **Visual Storytelling**

Key point

With digital visual effects it is possible for screenwriters to expand their minds and create any world they want for the screen, moving away from realism to fully use imagination.

Exercise: Exploring the impossible

Brainstorm ten highly imagined non-real worlds. Choose one that appeals to you. Write a 3–5 page script, pushing your imagination as far as possible. Ignore what may be impossible to realise, consider only what seems fun, enigmatic or dramatic. If it was purely animated, what would you do with the story? To produce this script on a low-budget, how could you exchange literal effects with suggestive storytelling?

Key point

Sound is often an invisible partner to visual storytelling, a highly evocative part of the film experience. Even on the page, screenwriters can use sound to create atmosphere, meaning and subtext, highlighting characters' inner states or dramatic tensions.

Exercise: Sound–image relationship

For each of the following locations, brainstorm ten interesting, unusual or dramatic sounds, and consider how their presence in a scene might affect tone, meaning, subtext and narrative possibilities:

- fish market
- hospital
- immaculate gardens
- examination hall
- submarine

- **Dialogues and Voices**

Key point

Screenwriters often develop their own style of writing; a personality recognisable to producers if not necessarily the audience. As an 'auteur', the screenwriter can point towards their work in two ways: profile of writing (ideas) and style of writing (voice). By studying various screenwriters, it can become clear what drives them in terms of what they want to say (ideas), and how they go about saying it (voice.)

Exercises: Personal voice

Writing your identity

Think about the kind of screenwriter you are. Look back at your work or plans to see if you can identify patterns of *ideas*. Are there key themes, issues, story worlds or agendas that your writing seems to encompass? Rationalise this by considering what has inspired you to write, and under what circumstances and summarise your writing profile.

Next look in depth at some of your writing (scenes, dialogue, visuals) to see whether you can identify patterns of *style* and *voice*. Do you have a particular set of archetypes you often draw upon? Do you work in particular genres? Does the dialogue replicate familiar worlds you have experienced? Again rationalise this by considering how elements of your personality shine through and make your writing voice unique.

Top tens

It can be enlightening to compare similarities and differences between what you like to write and like to watch and what this tells you about your voice. Write down your:

(1) Ten favourite films or TV dramas.
(2) Ten favourite fiction books.
(3) Ten favourite fairy tales or myths.

Pick one story in each category and write a short 50–100 word paragraph about it. What do you love about it? How does it make you feel reading/viewing it? What makes you come back to it again and again? Why have you chosen this over other stories for your top ten? What in this story relates to your voice as a writer in some way?

Look through the top tens to see if you can discover *common threads* or *themes* running through them. What do you discover about your tastes, passions and style? You may want to revisit your top tens occasionally; this can be very instructive, as we often assume our tastes stay the same when they can develop and change substantially.

Writer's statement

Write five hundred words about yourself as a screenwriter, including:

- Why you want to be a screenwriter?
- What kind of writer you are?
- What makes your voice special?
- What kind of career you want to follow as a writer?
- Why you deserve a place in the industry?
- How you feel about the industry in relation to you as a writer?

This is not a selling document for others, but a statement to yourself about your intentions, priorities and commitments. Write a new Writer's Statement, *without looking at your old one*, every six months. After you have finished, compare it to previous ones. How do you feel about similarities and differences between old and new? Keep the different versions, to revisit and reflect on progress and change.

Notes

Introduction

1. Here Harper argues that '[c]reative writing informs a *site of knowledge* that can be accessed and understood both formally and informally, that has a relationship with other sites of knowledge, and that gains substantially from keeping its borders open to movement outward and inward' (2006: 3). This ability to formulate an appropriate site of knowledge for, in this case screenwriting, is crucial if developments are to be made. Sustaining the approach of attaching 'other' theories to writing practice could be detrimental in screenwriting's pursuit for its own academic standing: 'to find the subject approached as if it is not a site of knowledge in its own right creates a situation in which the chances of achieving a 'justified true belief' are considerably diminished' (Ibid.).

8   Exploring Possibilities

1. Interestingly, the 'showrunner' of these sitcoms, Fred Barron, is an ex-patriot of America who had previous experience in US comedy.

9   Subjects: Ideas into Characters

1. See, for example, *The Independent's* 'Interview: Paul Allen, film Masters student at the International Film School Wales.' Here, Allen recalls that '[t]he link between psychology and drama is that you're telling stories about people. Particularly when you' re doing script writing, you're trying to work out the motivations of characters and how people work. We had a class by a script writing agent who actually advised people who wanted to study script writing to do a psychology degree first.' (Published 3rd July, 2007).
2. Indeed, Vogler's work is acknowledged as being heavily reliant upon Campbell's writing. In *The Writer's Journey*, Vogler specifically adapts Campbell's *The Monomyth* into a paradigm for screenwriters and contemporary storytellers. Although here we concentrate on contemporary writings, we would certainly recommend that anyone with a keen interest in screenwriting should read Campbell as a strong historical basis. Vladimir Propp's *Morphology of the Folktale* is also a seminal text

in terms of myth, story structure and character function, and highly recommended.

3. Paget (2004) notes generic functions of the dramadoc/docudrama. He argues that this can be: to re-tell events of national or international histories; to re-present careers of significant public figures; to portray issues of concern to national or international communities; and increasingly to focus on 'ordinary citizens' who have been thrust into the news (196). Our definition does not exclude that these functions exist, but because the nature of this discussion focuses upon the rhetoric of the form, we feel it more suitable to present a definition which specifies that whatever the content is, it is the context that is the same: to persuade, change, manipulate etc.

10   Structures and Narratives

1. For example, see Heath's (1996: xxxv–xliii) notes on *Poetics*. He talks at length about the problem of catharsis (or katharsis) in Aristotle's writing, and what it might have actually meant. See also Hiltunen (2002), whose understanding of Aristotle's catharsis translates into the bigger idea of 'proper pleasure'.

12   Dialogues and Voices

1. Think, for example, of the associations instantly made with names like Christopher Columbus, Martin Scorsese, Steven Spielberg and Peter Jackson.
2. Perkins and Stollery point towards the creative skills required of an editor, assuming similar functions to those of the screenwriter. These skills include 'sensitivity to the nuances and timing of performance [and] a feeling for dramatic construction and story structure' (2004: 37).
3. Other writers are used as brands names to accompany drama products, especially in television. Examples here could include Paul Abbott (*Clocking Off, Shameless, State of Play*) and Kay Mellor (*Playing the Field, Fat Friends, The Chase*). Here, the writers' names are used to denote a particular style or theme of writing (both, incidentally, Northern and gritty) which appeal to particular audiences.
4. It is interesting to note, however, that the writers mentioned by Davis have strong connections with the theatre, and one could argue that as such they already have established writerly personas and are attributed a sense of auteurship both by producers and themselves, enabling them to carry this status from one writerly tradition into another.
5. For example, John Fay, Carmel Morgan and Julie Jones are other *Coronation Street* writers who clearly have a distinctive voice which evades any sense of soap opera's traditionally viewed non-creativity.

Bibliography

Adams, M. (2001) *The Screenwriter's Survival Guide*, Victoria: Warner Books

Allen, P. (2007) 'Interview: Paul Allen, film Masters student at the International Film School Wales' in *The Independent*, 3rd July, 2007

Andermatt, P. (2003) *The Script Editor as Psychologist*, ScriptWriter Magazine (13)

Anon (2002) 'Everything We've Done is a Fraud' [Electronic Version] in *The Telegraph*, 26th April, 2002

Aristotle (1996) *Poetics*, (Trans. Malcolm Heath), London: Penguin

Aronson, L. (2001) *Screenwriting Updated: New (and Conventional) Ways of Writing for the Screen*, California: Silman-James Press

Beattie, K. (2004) *Documentary Screens: Nonfiction Film and Television*, Basingstoke: Palgrave Macmillan

Boulter, A. (2007) *Writing Fiction: Creative and Critical Approaches*, Basingstoke: Palgrave Macmillan

Campbell, J. (1993) *The Hero with a Thousand Faces*, London: Fontana

Caughie, J. (ed.) (2001) *Theories of Authorship*, London: Routledge

Creeber, G. (ed.) (2001) *The Television Genre Book*, London: BFI

Dancyger, K. and Rush, J. (2006) *Alternative Scriptwriting: Successfully Breaking the Rules* (4th ed.), Oxford: Focal Press

Davies, A. and Wistreich, N. (2005) *The UK Film Finance Handbook*, London: Netribution

Davis, R. (2003) *Writing Dialogue for Scripts* (2nd ed.), London: A & C Black

Davis, R. (2001) *Developing Characters for Script Writing*, London: A & C Black

Douglas, P. (2007) *Writing the TV Drama Series: How To Succeed as a Professional Writer in TV* (2nd ed.), California: Michael Wiese

Field, S. (2003) *The Definitive Guide to Screenwriting*, London: Ebury Press

Field, S. (1994) *Four Screenplay: Studies in the American Screenplay*, New York: Dell

Field, S. (1989) *Screenplay: The Foundations of Screenwriting*, New York: Dell

Friedman, J. (ed.) (2002) *Reality Squared: Televisual Discourse on the Real*, New Brunswick: Rutgers University Press

Goldberg, N. (1986) *Writing Down the Bones*, Boston: Shambhala

Grodal, T. (1997) *Moving Pictures: A New Theory of Film Genres, Feelings, and Cognition*, Oxford: Oxford University Press

Gulino, P. J. (2004) *Screenwriting: The Sequence Approach*, London: Continuum

Hallam, J. (2000) 'Power Plays: Gender, Genre and Lynda La Plante' in Jonathan Bignell and Stephen Lacey (eds.) *British Television Drama: Past, Present and Future*, Basingstoke: Palgrave Macmillan, pp. 140–9

Harper, G. (ed.) (2006) *Teaching Creative Writing*, London: Continuum

Harris, A. (2001) *An Interview with Shawn and Marlon Wayans: 'Getting the job done by making us laugh, again'*, available at http://blackfilm.com/20010713/features/i-shawnmarlonwayans.shtml (accessed 30th July, 2007)

Hiltunen, A. (2002) *Aristotle in Hollywood: Visual Stories that Work*, Bristol: Intellect

Holmes, S. and Jermyn, D. (2004) (eds.) *Understanding Reality Television*, London: Routledge

Horton, A. (1999) *Writing the Character-Centred Screenplay* (2nd ed.), Berkeley: University of California Press

Howard, D. (2004) *How to Build a Great Screenplay*, London: Souvenir Press

Hunter-Johnson, C. (2000) *Crafting Short Screenplays that Connect*, Woburn: Focal Press

Hutchings, P. (2004) *The Horror Film*, Harlow: Pearson

Hutzler, L. (2005) *Reaching Worldwide Audiences*, ScriptWriter Magazine (23)

Indick, W. (2004) *Psychology for Screenwriters: Building Conflict in Your Script*, California: Michael Wiese

Kilborn, R. (1994) 'Drama Over Lockerbie: A New Look at Television Drama-Documentaries', *Historical Journal of Film, Radio and Television*, vol. 14, no. 1, pp. 59–76

King, G. (2000) *Spectacular Narratives: Hollywood in the Age of the Blockbuster*, London: I.B. Tauris

Marlow, J. (2003) *Running the Show*, ScriptWriter Magazine (11)

McKee, R. (1999) *Story: Substance, Structure, Style and the Principles of Screenwriting*, London: Methuen

Melrose, A. (2007) 'Reading and Righting: Carrying on the "Creative Writing Theory" Debate' in *New Writing: The International Journal for the Practice and Theory of Creative Writing*, vol. 2, no. 2, pp. 109–17

Mittell, J. (2003) 'The "Classic Network System" in the US', in Michelle Hilmes (ed.) *The Television History Book*, London: BFI, pp. 44–9

Moritz, C. (2001) *Scriptwriting for the Screen*, London: Routledge

Nelson, R. (1997) *TV Drama in Transition*, Basingstoke: Palgrave Macmillan

Paget, D. (2004) 'Codes and Conventions of Dramadoc and Docudrama' in Robert C. Allen and Annette Hill (eds.) *The Television Studies Reader*, London: Routledge, pp. 196–208

Paget, D. (1998) *No Other Way To Tell It: Dramadoc/Docudrama on Television*, Manchester: Manchester University Press

Parker, P. (1999) *The Art and Science of Screenwriting* (2nd ed.), Exeter: Intellect

Perkins, R. and Stollery, M. (2004) *British Film Editors: The Heart of the Movie*, London: BFI

Propp, V. (1968) *The Morphology of the Folktale*, Austin: University of Texas Press

Rabiger, M. (2005) *Developing Story Ideas* (2nd ed.), Burlington: Focal Press

Rossio, T. (1997) *Story Molecule: Screenwriting Column 20*, available at http://www.wordplayer.com/columns/wp20.Story.Molecule.html (accessed 15th February, 2008)

Scher, L. (2003) *The Hitch Hiker's Guide to Genre*, available at http://www.scriptfactory.co.uk/go/News/Articles/Article_2.html (accessed 26th July, 2007)

Schepelern, P. (n.d.) *Film According to Dogma: Restrictions, Obstructions and Liberations*, available at http://www.dogme95.dk/news/interview/schepelern.htm (accessed 24th February, 2008)

Seger, L. (1990) *Creating Unforgettable Characters*, New York: Henry Holt

Seger, L. (1992) *The Art of Adaptation: Turning Fact and Fiction into Film*, New York: Henry Holt

Seger, L. (1994) *Making a Good Script Great* (2nd ed.), California: Samuel French

Seger, L. (1999) *Making a Good Writer Great: A Creativity Workbook for Screenwriters*, California: Silman-James Press

Seger, L. (2003) *Advanced Screenwriting: Raising Your Script to the Academy Award Level*, California: Silman-James Press

Sendall, J. (2003) *Developing With the Enemy*, ScriptWriter Magazine (8)

Smethurst, W. (2005) *Writing for Television*, Oxford: How To Books

Smith, M. (1995) *Engaging Characters: Fiction, Emotion, and the Cinema*, Oxford: Oxford University Press

Spicer, A. (2007) 'The Author as Author: Restoring the Screenwriter to British Film History' in James Chapman, Mark Glancy and Sue Harper (eds.) *The New Film History: Sources, Methods, Approaches*, Basingstoke: Palgrave Macmillan, pp. 89–103

Taylor, T. (1999) *The Big Deal*, New York: William Morrow & Co

Vinterberg, T. (n.d) *Why Dogme?*, available at http://www.dogme95.dk (accessed 24th February, 2008)

Vogler, C. (1999) *The Writer's Journey: Mythic Structure for Storytellers and Screenwriters* (2nd ed.), London: Pan

Weston, J. (1996) *Directing Actors*, California: Michael Wiese

Filmography/Television

The 40 Year Old Virgin (2005)
After You've Gone (2007–)
Alien (1979)
American Beauty (1999)
Annie Hall (1977)
Auf Wiedersehen Pet (1983–2004)
Bad Girls (1999–2006)
The Banger Sisters (2002)
Batman (1989)
Bean (1997)
Beautiful Thing (1996)
Before You Go (2002)
Big Brother (2000–)
The Big Lebowski (1998)
Birthday Girl (2002)
Black Books (2000)
Blood Simple (1984)
The Bourne Identity (2002)
The Bourne Supremacy (2004)
The Bourne Ultimatum (2007)
Brat Camp (2005–)
The Bridges of Madison County (1995)
Brief Encounter (1945)
Brokeback Mountain (2005)
Brookside (1982–2003)
Charlie's Angel (2004)
Citizen Kane (1941)
City of God (2002)
Clapham Junction (2007)
Coronation Street (1960–)
Date Movie (2006)
Deadwood (2004–2006)
Dolores Claiborne (1995)
Driving School (1997)
Drop Dead Gorgeous (1999)
Epic Movie (2007)
Father Ted (1995–8)
The Fast Show (1994–2001)
Festen (1998)
Fight Club (1999)

The Fishmonger (2002)
Footballers' Wives (2002–)
Four Weddings and a Funeral (1994)
Friends (1994–2004)
Gimme, Gimme, Gimme (1999–2001)
Glengarry, Glen Ross (1992)
The Green Mile (1999)
Groundhog Day (1993)
Halloween (1978)
Harry Potter (2001–)
Holiday Showdown (2003–)
Hollyoaks (1995–)
The Hours (2002)
How to Tell When a Relationship is Over (2003)
I Know What You Did Last Summer (1997)
James Bond (1962–)
Jaws (1975)
Kitchen Stories (2003)
The Last Kiss Goodnight (1996)
Little Angels (2004–)
Location, Location, Location (2001–)
The Lord of the Rings (Trilogy) (2001–3)
Lost in Translation (2003)
Love Actually (2003)
Love for Sale (2005)
Magnolia (1999)
Man Bites Dog (1992)
Mean Girls (2004)
Meet the Parents (2000)
Memento (2000)
Misery (1990)
Monster (2003)
Muriel's Wedding (1994)
My Family (2000–)
Not Another Teen Movie (2001)
Notting Hill (1999)
Paris Je T'aime (2006)
Pirates of the Caribbean (2003)
Porridge (1974–7)
Property Ladder (2001–)
The Return (2003)
Scary Movie (2000)
Scream (1996)
Scrubs (2001–)
Sex and the City (1998–2004)
The Simpsons (1989–)
Sin City (2005)
Six Feet Under (2001–2005)
The Sopranos (1999–2007)

The Sound of Music (1965)
Strictly Ballroom (1992)
Supernanny (2004–)
Telling Lies (2000)
There's Something About Mary (1998)
Tillsammans/Together (2000)
Titanic (1997)
Tootsie (1982)
Toy Story (1995)
Ugly Betty (2006–)
Veronique (2002)
Von Trapped (2004)
The West Wing (1999–2006)
Whatever Happened to the Likely Lads? (1973–4)
What Not To Wear (2001–)
When I was Falling ... (1999)
Wife Swap (2003–)
The Wizard of Oz (1939)
Wonder Boys (2000)
You Are What You Eat (2004–)
X-Men (2000)

Index